CW00459810

Visor!™

I Didn't Know You Could Do That...™

Neil J. Salkind

SYBEX®

San Francisco • Paris • Düsseldorf • Soest • London

Associate Publisher: Roger Stewart
Contracts and Licensing Manager: Kristine O'Callaghan
Acquisitions & Developmental Editor: Diane Lowery
Editors: Susan Berge, Patrick J. Peterson
Technical Editor: James Hromadka
Book Designers: Franz Baumhackl, Kate Kaminski
Electronic Publishing Specialists: Nila Nichols, Susie Hendrickson
Production Editor: Leslie Higbee
Proofreaders: Dave Nash, Nancy Riddiough
Indexer: Matthew Spence
CD Coordinator: Kara Schwartz
CD Technicians: Ginger Warner, Keith McNeil
Cover Designer/Illustrator: Daniel Ziegler
Cover Photograph: PhotoDisc

Library of Congress Card Number: 00-102077
ISBN: 0-7821-2782-7

Manufactured in the United States of America
10 9 8 7 6 5 4 3 2 1

To the River City Sharks

Acknowledgments

All these good people helped me create this book for you, our readers:

Great thanks and appreciation to Diane Lowery and Roger Stewart at Sybex for giving me the opportunity to complete this project and for their guidance throughout its development. Thank you also to the editorial and production team: Susan Berge and Patrick Peterson, Editors; Leslie Higbee, Production Editor; Dave Nash and Nancy Riddiough, Proofreaders; Nila Nichols, Electronic Publishing Specialist; Kara Schwartz, Keith McNeil, and Ginger Warner, the CD team; and great thanks to James Hromadka, the Technical Editor who kept me honest.

My warmest thanks to David and Sherry Rogelberg for giving me the opportunity to write this book and for everything else they do. And of course, always for Sara.

Contents

COMPUTE THIS!: A CALCULATOR FOR EVERYTHING AND EVERYONE

HOURS OF FUN: GAMES, GAMES, GAMES . . . 209

WHAT A PRETTY PICTURE: GRAPHICS AND DESIGN 225

APPENDIX A: WHERE IN THE WORLD TO FIND ALL THE VISOR PROGRAMS YOU COULD EVER WANT . 231

APPENDIX B: THE BEST PALMPILOT APPLICATION LIST IN THE UNIVERSE 237

Introduction

Now that you finally have your Visor ☺, imagine using it to do any of these things:

1. Find out if you should sell your Amazon stock

2. Play Tetris until the wee hours of the morning

3. Customize your shopping list

4. Calculate your mortgage payoff

Imagine no more. The Visor, the new hand-held personal digital assistant from Handspring, Inc. can do this and more. And besides all kinds of nifty features, perhaps the best thing about the Visor is that it uses the same operating system (or OS) as the wildly popular line of 3Com's PalmPilot devices. That's right. Any program that runs on the Palm can run on the Visor (with the exception of special hardware-related programs such as the Palm VII wireless features for example).

Your Visor does more than just allow you to record telephone numbers and memos and track a list of errands and tasks. In fact, it's a business tool, a traveling companion, even a hand-held game player. It's a personal digital assistant that can do more things than you are aware of. This book shows you just what some of those things are and how to do them.

And if you're really lucky, then you have one of the Springboard modules that snap into the back of your Visor. These modules are the defining feature that sets the Visor apart from the PalmPilot. For example, you can turn your Visor into a cell phone, back up all your Visor data, or even use the GPS (global positioning satellite) module to find your longitude and latitude any place on the planet!

Visor! I Didn't Know You Could Do That… shows you some of the best, easily available Visor applications. They can increase your productivity in business, make your traveling more enjoyable, and give you hours of fun playing games. You'll find calculators that compute the correct tip for each person in your dinner party, databases that can help manage your book collection, and—if you get truly bored with all this—you can read one of Tom Swift's great adventures—all on your Visor, whether you have the standard or the deluxe version.

What's in This Book

Visor! I Didn't Know You Could Do That... contains an in-depth description of 98 different Visor applications that best represent the capability of the Visor. These applications can be used with any Visor that uses the OS3 (Operating System 3) or later. You can download new versions of the Palm OS (which is what the Visor uses) at Palm Computing located at `http://palmpilot.3com.com/custsupp/downloads/indexdl.html` on the Internet.

The different applications in *Visor! I Didn't Know You Could Do That...* are organized in the following categories:

◆ Making Your Visor Work Even Better: Tools and Utilities

◆ Organizing Everything: Databases and Information Management

◆ Compute This!: A Calculator for Everything and Everyone

◆ It's Your Business!

◆ Keeping Time: Clocks and Calendars

◆ Communications Anywhere, Anytime

◆ Say What You Mean and Mean What You Say

◆ Lifelong Learning and Your Visor: Education

◆ Healthy Mind, Healthy Body

◆ Your Traveling Guide

◆ Too Cool for Words

◆ Hours of Fun: Games, Games, Games

◆ What a Pretty Picture: Graphics and Design

Each of the categories contains a number of Visor applications that have been tried-and-true tested by a crack team of fun loving, Visor-loving experts (the author and his family and friends), who can endorse each one as working as claimed and *very* useful. Once you find an application that you like, just download it to your Visor and it's there for you to use.

Besides the 98 different applications that are described in the main part of the book, there are more contained on the CD-ROM that accompanies the book. Each of these can be easily downloaded to your Visor.

The Application Descriptions

Each description of the programs in the book and on the CD-ROM contain the following information:

Name of Program   The name as it appears on the Internet or as the developer or manufacturer indicates. Sometimes names are followed by version numbers such as 1.0 or 1.1. It's important to know the version number if you need to contact technical support. It's also important also since you always want to upgrade to the latest version.

E-Mail Address   The address where you can write for more information about the application should you have any questions or comments (which are for the most part always welcome).

Web Address   The Web site URL (or Internet address) where you can download the program, find additional information about the application, other applications offered by the same company, online manuals (if available), and often tons of other goodies you might want to consider.

Version   The official version of the software that was available at the time of this printing.

Type of Software   We mention three types throughout the book. They are shareware, commercial, or freeware.

Cost   The price to register or buy the product, if any, at the time of this printing.

Description   Details about what the application does and its special features and such.

Getting Started with...   This is just the basics on how to use the application.

Important Commands   These will allow you to see at a glance what command performs what function.

Try before You Buy

Each of the software programs that you find on the CD-ROM accompanying *Visor! I Didn't Know You Could Do That…* falls into one of three categories:

Commercial Software This is the software you pay full price for through some kind of a distributor, at the local store or national chain, or directly on the Internet. (Commercial software for the Visor averages about $40 at the time of this printing.)

Shareware This is software that has been developed and is widely available based on the philosophy that if a good product is introduced to the market place at a fair price, then users will be willing to pay a nominal fee for its use.

Shareware got started when individuals realized that commercial software was too expensive and the channels through which it was distributed were inefficient. Shareware developers encourage users to share applications with other users, that way, the potential for more registered users increases.

The way shareware works (and the majority of the programs in this book and on the disk are shareware) is as follows:

1. You download the program you want to try

2. If you like it, you send the requested fee to the developer

Why pay? Simple. If the developer continues to be paid (and rewarded) for his or her efforts, the results are a better version of the original application. So for $10 (about the average shareware price for Visor applications), you get an application that does what you want, the developer benefits for his or her hard work, and you are informed of future upgrades and improvements. Everybody wins. So if you download Visor applications, and try them, and if you like them, pay the small fee and keep a nice example of capitalism alive.

Freeware This software is absolutely free for the asking and taking. The developer expects nothing in return save for your appreciation for a fun and useful product. Freeware sometimes becomes shareware once it has found its place in the market.

Getting New Applications

This book brings you 98 descriptions and numerous other applications that you can use on your Visor, and there are thousands more available on the Internet. It's amazingly easy to get and to use each and every one. In this section of the Introduction, I'll show you how to get an application from your desktop computer to your Visor. Then I'll show you how to get a program from the Internet to your desktop.

From the Disk to Your Desktop

To transfer an application from your desktop, follow these steps. These apply no matter where the application files are located—be it on your hard drive, a floppy drive, or on the CD-ROM that accompanies this book. Most application files will come to you compressed or "zipped." If this is the case, you must first unzip them using an application such as WinZip that I will discuss shortly.

NOTE We're assuming that you have already installed the Visor software, your Visor cradle is attached and working and that you know how to HotSync or transfer files from your Visor to your desktop computer.

1. Locate the file you want to download. Visor files almost always have the following extensions or three letter characters after the name of the file: .prc or .pdb. If you see a file with this extension (such as doodle.prc), you know that it is a Visor application.

2. Click Start ➤ Programs ➤ Palm Pilot Desktop ➤ Install Tool and you will see the dialog box shown below.

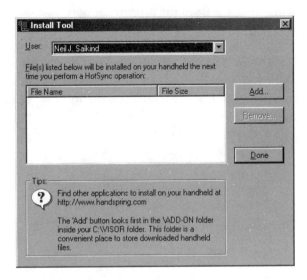

3. Click Add and locate the file you want to install.

4. Click Open.

5. Click Done.

6. Press the HotSync button on your Visor and the files that you identified will be transferred from the desktop to your Visor.

The newly installed programs are ready to use; when you tap the Applications button on your Visor, they should appear in the screen.

From the Internet to Your Desktop

To use any of the millions of cool Internet sites with Visor applications available, you first have to download them from the Internet to your desktop, and then transfer them from your desktop to your Visor (which we just told you about above). Files on the Internet are usually in an compressed form, so the one other step you need to take after they are downloaded is to expand the file. I'll show you how to do that shortly.

To download a file from the Internet, follow these steps:

1. Locate the file on the Internet.

2. Download the file. You do this by either clicking the filename or clicking a phrase such as "Download Now." Sometimes you just click an icon that represents the file. In any case, you'll see some indication, as you do below, of the file being transferred from a remote connection to your computer.

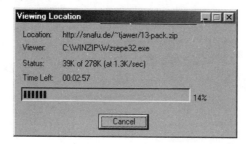

3. Windows may show you a Save dialog box and ask you to indicate where you want the saved file located or it will use the default location that you have previously specified. Use the Browse button to find the folder where you want the file downloaded to, or just use the default location.

4. Click Open and the file will be saved to that location. Most Visor application files are very small and, depending upon the speed of your Internet connection, can be downloaded very quickly (almost faster than you can see).

5. Once the file is downloaded, it is read to be HotSync'd to your Visor, unless it has to be unzipped.

Using WinZip

WinZip is an ingenious product. It takes a file and compresses it to a fraction of its size, making the transfer from one computer to another (such as over the Internet) much, much faster. While WinZip (the shareware or evaluation version of which is contained on the CD-ROM) is very powerful and has many different features, simply uncompressing a file is relatively uncomplicated.

WinZip comes with an easy-to-use Wizard (shown below) which works with files that you are downloading from the Internet. The WinZip Wizard automates almost all of the work normally associated with downloading compressed files from the Internet. When you click an archive (which appears as the zipped file icon) using Netscape Navigator or Microsoft Internet Explorer, WinZip takes over and automatically moves the downloaded file to the download folder (which is initially set to c:\download) and then opens the file.

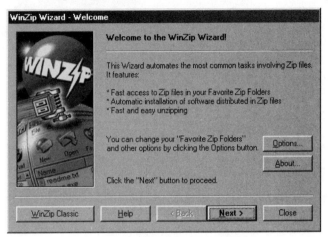

You can also right-click the archives zip file icon (whatever.zip), click the Extract To option, and compressed files will be extracted to the same directory in which they are currently located. You're then ready to install the Visor program as we described above.

NOTE   When you unzip a file, you may just reveal a .prc file for your Visor, but you may reveal much more. Some Visor programs are accompanied by user manuals or even HTML formatted files that when clicked, deliver you to a Web address all about the files you downloaded. So, don't be surprised to find some new and cool stuff beyond just the Visor program you want.

That's it! All you need to know to get started with *Visor! I Didn't Know You Could Do That....* The only way you can maximize the fun you can have with this book is to download the applications and actually use them. So, go to it and have a ball!

Making Your Visor Work Even Better: Tools and Utilities

This first section focuses on tools and utilities that will make your Visor life easier—from keeping track of how much memory your Visor has left for new applications to backing up all that valuable data you entered this afternoon at the company holiday party.

So while the Visor is a great little personal helper all by itself, it becomes even more useful (and even more fun) when you have the following set of tools helping you work more efficiently.

1 Keep Track of Your Utilities: FPS Utility Pro

FPS Utility Pro, Version 4.1

www.fps.com

Shareware: $15

FPS Utility Pro is a one-stop shopping, Palm-certified utility that brings you all the important info and tools you need to run, understand, and keep up with your Visor. The Main FPS Utility Screen provides vital statistics about your Palm Computing Platform Device, including free memory battery status (to 1/1000th of a volt), and sleep status (four, five, and ten minutes, as well as never sleep—which is a real battery-eater). (All this information is updated about every two seconds.) Tap the CardInfo button and get additional information about memory, or tap the HotSync button and find out more about HotSync than you might ever have wanted to know. Then there are even more sophisticated and useful sources of information, including a list (which can be easily sorted) of all the databases on your Visor, a set of buttons for managing these databases (such as a Trash and Beam button), and simple delete and export tools. It's a complete package and would be a good choice as the first thing you load when you start adding new stuff to your Visor.

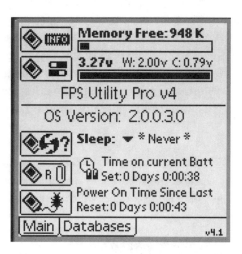

Getting Started with FPS Utility Pro

To use FPS Utility Pro, tap the Main or Database button on the opening screen to view the general status of the operating system or to work with one of the existing system databases. However, unless you are fairly experienced with the Palm OS, it's best to leave the database manipulation activities to the experts.

2 Install Operating System Extensions: HackMaster

HackMaster, Version 0.9

www.daggerware.com/hackmstr.htm

Shareware: $5

HackMaster allows you to use other programs designed for the Visor that are created as "hack extensions," such as FindHack or SwitchHack. A hack extension is a small program that operates with HackMaster. More important, HackMaster provides an easy-to-use applications management tool and allows you to install and uninstall PalmOS extensions in any order without restarting. In the words of the developer, Edward Keyes, Hack-Master "provides a standard method for managing, installing, and uninstalling system extensions, and many other third-party developers have embraced it as the system-patching method of choice."

NOTE Many of the applications mentioned in this book require Hack-Master, including FindHack and SwitchHack.

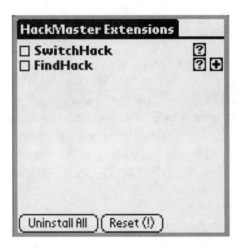

Getting Started with HackMaster

Follow these steps to install extensions with HackMaster:

1. Install the hack extensions you want to use with your Visor.

2. Open HackMaster.

3. In the HackMaster screen, tap the check box to the left of the application you want to use.

4. Tap the + sign to configure the extension, or tap the ? sign for help.

3 Search with Wildcard Symbols: FindHack

FindHack, Version 2.8

`http://perso.wanadoo.fr/fpillet/`

Shareware: $6

Your Visor has a Find function that is limited in usefulness. It can find a string of letters, but if you don't have all the detail (like all the characters) to find what you need, this isn't enough. FindHack can search for letters that are contained within a word and supports that essential search feature known as *wildcard symbols* (such as *). Wildcard symbols each do something different. An asterisk (*) takes the place of any number of letters. For example, if you wanted to find all occurrences of words that start with "ar," then ar* would come up with anything from artist to Archimedes! A question mark (?) takes the place of only one letter. For example, if you wanted to find all the files that start with "chap" and are followed with a single-digit number, you would search for chap?

FindHack also tracks the last six searches you have done so you can easily go back and review previous searches, and it lets you save four permanent searches to find recurring information again. When you install it, FindHack replaces the Find feature (the lower-right screen button on your Visor), as shown in the following graphic. Just enter the terms you need, tap OK, and let FindHack do the rest.

To use FindHack, you need HackMaster, which you'll find on the companion CD-ROM.

Getting Started with FindHack

Here are the steps you need to use FindHack:

1. Tap HackMaster on the Visor Applications screen.

2. Tap the FindHack check box.

3. Tap the + sign to the right of FindHack.

4 Switch When and How You Want: SwitchHack

SwitchHack, Version 1.6

www.deskfree.com

Shareware: $5

Your Windows or Mac operating system allows you to switch from one application to another (called *multitasking*) with a simple tap or Alt+Tab key combination, but who would have thought that you could have the same capability on your Visor? Well, the fine people behind SwitchHack did. SwitchHack is a HackMaster extension that allows you to move between two programs with a single stroke in the Graffiti (or handwriting) area. You use a pop-up menu to see the last 10 applications opened and then use the menu to make any of these applications active.

Version 1.6 offers lots of cool features:

◆ Work on one project, look up an address or a phone number, and then return to where you were.

◆ Have two programs active simultaneously.

◆ Copy text and create a shortcut for it, and then switch back and use the copied text again.

◆ HotSync and then return to the program you were originally running.

◆ Boss coming? Make a speedy switch from PacMan to something more serious.

In addition, SwitchHack has an instant menu of the 10 most recently run applications for you to select by name, and you can return to the last viewed/edited address feature when switching back to the Address Book application.

N O T E   SwitchHack requires that you have HackMaster installed. You can find HackMaster on the companion CD-ROM.

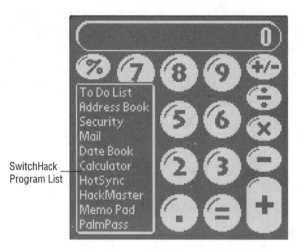

SwitchHack
Program List

Getting Started with SwitchHack

To use SwitchHack, remember that you must first install HackMaster. After installing SwitchHack, you will only see the HackMaster icon on your Visor application screen. Follow these steps to activate SwitchHack:

1. Tap HackMaster and you'll see SwitchHack (and any other Hack-Master extensions).

2. Tap the check box for SwitchHack and run the programs you want. When you are ready to switch, drag from the application button to the Graffiti area using the stylus or your finger.

3. If you want to see the set of applications that you have been using and which you can instantly tap and select, drag the Menu button up to the Applications button to open the menu. Now you can tap away.

5 Never Lose Data Again: BackupBuddy

BackupBuddy, Version 1.1

www.backupbuddy.com

Shareware: $29.95

There are two kinds of people: those who have lost data and those who will. When you HotSync, data from the Visor is synchronized with your PC, but many third-party applications (such as ones in this book and on the accompanying CD) are not synced. BackupBuddy takes care of this task and automatically backs up anything that is not included in the normal one-button HotSync. Should you experience a data loss (such as if you changed batteries but took too long), a simple HotSync will do the job. BackupBuddy lives in your desktop machine, not on your Visor, and unlike many other Visor applications, BackupBuddy comes with an extensive, complete, and well-written manual. Bravo!

BackupBuddy's nifty features include

◆ The ability to back up your Visor to more than one desktop computer

◆ A view of the backup status as it progresses

◆ Support for multiple users

◆ Infrared HotSync support

◆ Memory savings, because there is no need for a resident program on your Visor

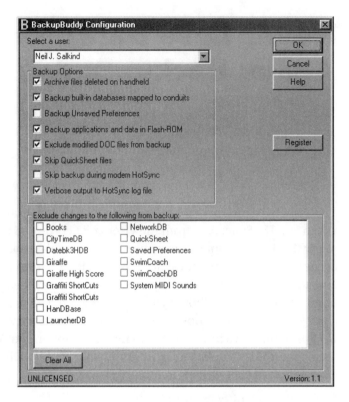

Getting Started with BackupBuddy

Follow these steps to use BackupBuddy:

1. Install BackupBuddy as you would any Windows application.

2. Indicate whether you want your Visor to overwrite desktop files, desktop files to overwrite your Visor, or neither.

3. Press the HotSync button with the Visor in its cradle, and your files are backed up.

6 Print Directly from Your Visor Using Infrared: PalmPrint

PalmPrint, Version 1

www.stevenscreek.com/pilot/palmprint.shtml

Shareware: $39.95

If you really want to be a mobile girl or guy and use your Visor for just about everything, PalmPrint is an invaluable tool. It allows you to print directly from your Visor and, in some cases (such as with the Visor III or V, which have infrared capability), without a cable even being attached. Now that's cool. Your PalmPrint can now print memos, lists, or anything else it copies to the Visor Clipboard from another application (such as Word or Excel). What's more, PalmPrint comes with a modified version of the standard Palm Mail application (Mail/P), which can print e-mails, and a limited version of SnailMailer, which prints envelopes and mailing labels. PalmPrint also supports automatic word wrapping, Portrait and Landscape mode, a configurable number of characters per line and lines per page, and more.

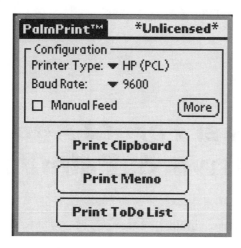

Getting Started with PalmPrint

To print using PalmPrint, follow these steps:

1. Load the document you want to print into the Visor Clipboard.

2. Start PalmPrint by tapping the PalmPrint icon.

3. Configure the printer.

4. Tap Print Clipboard.

Check out this table for all the commands needed for PalmPrint.

Menu	Command	Shortcut	What It Does
Options	Check IR Communications	None	Checks the infrared ports setup
	About PalmPrint	None	Tells you all about PalmPrint

TIP PalmPrint works with many different printers, such as HP, Epson, Canon, and so on. But don't overlook perhaps the coolest feature of any Visor program: To print your file, you just need to beam it using your Visor. Look, Ma—no cables!

7 Never Forget Another Password: PalmPass

PalmPass, Version 1

http://www.palmgear.com/software/showsoftware
.cfm?sid=684458200001121924143ProdID=5683

Freeware

How in the world do you keep all those passwords straight? First, it's the broker, then *The New York Times* online, then access to one of the many airlines that require a password to buy tickets. One way to keep all your passwords in order is the simple but effective (and free) Visor utility called PalmPass. As you can see in the following list, PalmPass allows you to track all types of passwords. You can also include general information to keep things from becoming chaotic, such as the title, login, password, and URL. You can edit password information and use the quick-entry feature to place your passwords in one of the following categories:

- ◆ Encrypted file
- ◆ PIN
- ◆ Service password
- ◆ System password
- ◆ WWW site
- ◆ Other

WARNING Be careful about storing passwords on your Visor or any other device you keep close to your person. Unless you lock your Visor (tap Security and provide a password), your stolen Visor is a thief's opportunity to attack any password, from your ATM to your gold club brokerage account!

Getting Started with PalmPass

PalmPass is simple to use. Just follow these steps:

1. Tap New.

2. Enter the password and associated information.

3. Tap OK.

You can review your passwords by tapping either end of the arrow on the screen.

8 Install Visor Programs in a Mouse-Tap: Stall

Stall, Version 1

www.tauschke.com/html/start_e_.html

Freeware

If you're having fun with all the applications contained on the CD-ROM that comes with this book, get ready for Stall to make things even easier. Stall is a Windows-based installation program that allows you to install one or more of your Visor programs at a time with just one tap of the mouse (by pressing the Shift+Tap or Ctrl+Tap key combination). Just imagine how much time this will save!

Getting Started with Stall

Follow these steps to get up and running:

1. Download and install Stall on your PC.

2. Open Windows Explorer and locate the Visor program (it'll have a .prc or .pdb extension, or it'll be a Zip file) that you want to install.

3. Right-tap the icon, and select Send To ➤ PalmPilot.

4. HotSync, and the program or programs are installed.

9 Purge Duplicate Entries from Your Visor: UnDupe

UnDupe, Version 1

www.stevenscreek.com/pilot/dodownload.html

Shareware: $7.95

It happens to every Visor user. You find that all the entries in your Visor are duplicated, even quadruplicated, and you end up with thousands instead of hundreds of entries. What a drag it is to delete each entry one at a time. UnDupe removes the duplicates with a tap of one button. You can choose where you want the duplicates deleted from—the Date Book, Address Book, Memo Pad, or To Do List, or you can tap the All button and the program will delete duplicates from each of the four major applications.

There's even a Find Only mode so you can have UnDupe tell you how many duplicates it finds in each database before they are deleted.

UnDupe works by comparing characteristics of the saved items. For example, for Date Book items, it compares the date, the start and end times, the alarms, the item itself, and any attached note. It does a similar type of comparison for the other major Visor applications, as well. The only way an item can be deleted is if it is an exact match with another item, although if UnDupe finds two entries that are identical, but one has an attached note, it will delete the one without the attached note. UnDupe is even smart enough to keep two entries that are exactly the same in different categories.

Getting Started with UnDupe

Follow these steps to free yourself from duplicated entries:

1. Tap the application for which you want duplicates removed (Date Book, Address Book, Memo Pad, To Do List, or All).

2. Tap the option you want to use:

◆ The Find Duplicates option finds all the duplicates.

◆ The Find and Remove option finds all the duplicates and removes them.

◆ The Fast Search option works quickly but may miss duplicates in the Date Book.

◆ The Exhaustive option finds everything but is slow.

10 Attach a Keyboard to Your Visor: GoType! Pro

GoType! Pro

www.landware.com

Commercial software: $79.95

If you've ever been reluctant to use your Visor for entering lots of text, fear no more. GoType! Pro is a great keyboard for the Visor that lets you enter information as easily and quickly as you can type, with no cables to connect and no extra batteries. As for features, GoType! Pro is full of them, including

◆ Six user-defined function keys

◆ Rapid access to 24 applications

◆ Special keys for commands and shortcuts

◆ Lightweight keyboard (only 11 ounces)

◆ Very compact size, but a large enough keyboard to make it actually useful

◆ A built-in USB port for direct synchronization from the keyboard

This is no kidding around stuff. GoType! Pro really works. And if you want to get extra fancy, LandWare also offers a carrying case (leather for you Visor owners with deep pockets) and a keyboard protector as extras.

Getting Started with GoType! Pro

Here's all you need to do to start using GoType! Pro:

1. Install the driver on your PC (or Mac).

2. HotSync.

3. Place your Visor in the cradle on top of the GoType! Pro keyboard and then type away.

11 Create Your Very Own Visor Applications: PalmFactory

PalmFactory, Version 1

www.alcita.com/palmfactory

Freeware

Ever wonder how those smart people get those cool Visor applications to work in the first place? How do they create those neat games, utilities, and applications that make the Visor so much fun and so useful? It's not rocket science—it's the PalmFactory.

This is not a Visor application, but rather a Windows 95 and 98 application you use to create a Visor application (with a .pfa extension) and then HotSync to your Visor for testing and use. The PalmFactory Web site is full of terrific tools and examples to help you. For instance, by examining the source code for the application, you can get a good idea of how to modify and create your own applications. Among the examples, you'll find both the working .prc Visor file, as well as the .pfa file. You will also find

◆ A relational database

◆ MileageCalc, for tracking travel sites

◆ MyCar!, for computing and storing vehicle usage

◆ TimeCard, for recording time spent on tasks

◆ PalmProducer, a contact manager

The home page also offers QuickTips, a tutorial, and a discussion group. If you want to get into creating Visor applications, this is the perfect place to start. In the following graphic, you can see how an application consists of a variety of forms, each of which is created independently.

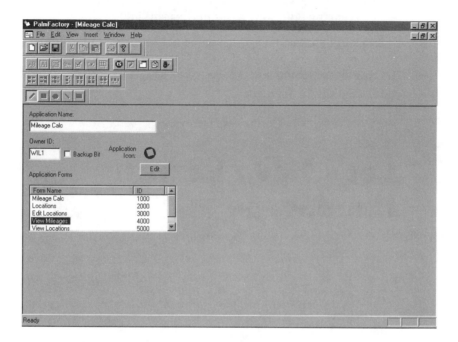

Getting Started with PalmFactory

It's way beyond the scope of this book to teach you how to use PalmFactory, but we can at least guide you through a few steps to get started. There is an extraordinarily helpful PalmFactory Cheat Sheet (courtesy of LaDeana Dockery) you can download as an Adobe file from the home page.

Here's how to create a new application:

1. Click the New button in the PalmFactory main page.

2. Provide a title for the application that is no more than 32 characters.

3. Enter a 4-character owner ID. If you plan on distributing the application, you need to register it at www.palm.com.

Once you have created an application, you can create a check box, one of many different elements that can be included in almost any application.

1. Click the check box icon in the PalmFactory toolbar.

2. Double-click the element you want to create the check box for to reveal the Edit Control Properties window.

3. Complete the field ID using a 4-character identifier.

Once a file is created and is saved as a .pda file, it is HotSync-ed to your Visor, and you're in business.

12 Let's Have Launch: HandScape

HandScape, Version 1

www.palmmate.com/handscape/index.html

Freeware

Don't trouble yourself with all those extra taps! HandScape will not only provide you with a default opening screen of your own design but also allow you to open, with only one tap on your Visor, the application in the group you want. If you want to know what meetings you have today or whether it's time to order that Valentine's Day present, install HandScape and configure it to do just that.

What HandScape has to offer that is so unique is what they call a LiveDesktop, where *views* (designed by you) are provided. These views can be general (such as the time and date) or quite specific, such as the next scheduled meeting you have. Once installed, you have the following views available:

◆ The Analog Clock View displays the time in an old-fashioned clock with an old-fashioned second hand (how retro).

◆ The Digital Clock View displays the time and date in digits (how boring).

◆ The Battery Status View displays the battery status to help you avoid running out of gas (how important).

◆ The DateBook View displays the upcoming events from your Date-Book (how handy).

◆ The ToDo View will display the top items from your To Do List. It will display a dim light bulb if you have no items in the To Do List, and a bright light bulb if you do (how cool).

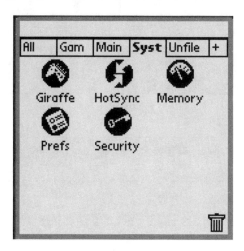

Getting Started with HandScape

HandScape does lots of cool things. One of them is starting up an application that will automatically launch when you turn on your Visor. Here's how to do it:

1. Tap the Menu button.

2. Tap Options.

3. Tap Preferences.

4. Select an application as your start-up application.

This chart shows a couple of commands you need to know to use HandScape.

Menu	Command	Shortcut	What It Does
File	PalmInfo	/I	Provides memory-use information about your Palm operating system
	OpenViews Manager	None	Allows you to manage and beam views
	Show Hidden Views	None	Shows you what views are hidden
	Exit to Palm SO	None	Exits to the Palm operating system
Edit	Undo	/U	Undoes most recent operation
	Copy	/X	Copies information
	Cut	/C	Removes information
	Paste	/P	Pastes information
	Select All	/A	Selects all information
	Keyboard	/K	Uses the keyboard to enter information
	Graffiti	/G	Uses Graffiti to enter information

Menu	Command	Shortcut	What It Does
Options	About HandScape	None	Tells you all about HandScape
	Preferences	/R	Sets preferences
	Help	/H	Gets help
	Beam HandScape	/B	Beams HandScape information to another Visor
	How to Register	None	Registers HandScape
	Registration	None	Registers HandScape

Organizing
Everything

There used to be a children's television series that featured a fellow named Stuffman who would tote around a huge duffel bag filled with—what else?—stuff. Part of the reason he would always be schlepping this collection around is because he had no place to put it and no way to organize it. That's not a problem for Visor users like you.

In this section and on the accompanying CD-ROM, I'll show you many different ways to use your Visor to organize, retrieve, and view information, from a powerful general database application (HanDBase) to a customizable list for tracking purchases at the supermarket or anywhere else you shop.

13 Install a Powerful Database onto Your Visor: HanDBase

HanDBase, Version 2

www.ddhsoftware.com

Shareware: $19.99

Databases are one of the most popular applications on any personal or business computer. You know that CD collection you have strewn all over the house? With a database, you can organize your collection's information by artist, title, date, or another category. How about your collection of Beanie Babies or the names and addresses of all your important business contacts? Want to put them in one place in any order? Then create a database to help keep your information organized the way you want. For the Visor, the database I recommend is HanDBase. With HanDBase you can

◆ Filter records so you view only the records you want.

◆ Use calculated fields for computing special values.

◆ Sort any field in ascending or descending order just by tapping the field name.

- Create reports on selected fields and see the min, max, average, sum, and other simple statistics.
- Export records to the Memo Pad.
- Search fields for a word or expression.
- Use pop-ups to ease data entry.
- Incorporate images into your database.
- Create links to jump to other databases.

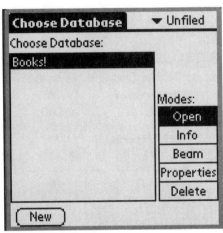

In addition to all of the above, the new version of HanDBase comes with a collection of *applets,* or small applications, such as Gas Mileage Tracker, Medical/Patient tracking, CheckBook Applet, Courier/Delivery Tracker, Real Estate Database, and Shopping List Applet. Who could ask for anything more?

Getting Started with HanDBase

Here's how to create a simple database for your CD collection, including artist, title, date of release, and purchase price.

1. Tap New.

2. Enter the name of the database.

3. Tap the Field 1 button.

4. Name the field **Artist**.

5. Specify the type of field from the ▼ menu.

6. Tap OK.

7. Repeat steps 3 through 6 to specify a new field for title, date, price, or another category.

8. Tap OK.

9. Open the database by selecting it, and tap New to create a record.

This table shows some basic commands that will get you organized in no time.

Menu	Option	Shortcut	What It Does
Prefs	Preferences	/R	Defines how you want the records to appear
	DB Properties	/D	Edits the basic structure of the database
Actions	Sorting	/S	Sorts the records in the database
	Filters	/F	Selects records from the database according to specified criteria
	Export Records	/E	Exports records
	Print Records	/P	Prints records
	Beam Records	/B	Beams records
	Delete Records	/D	Deletes records
	Run Report	/R	Begins report creation
	Copy Template	/O	Copies a template of a database for use in a new database
	Delete Database	/K	Deletes a database

Menu	Option	Shortcut	What It Does
Move	To Top	/T	Goes to the top of the database
	To Bottom	/B	Goes to the bottom of the database
	To Right	/I	Moves to the right
	To Left	/L	Moves to the left
	Page Right	/H	Moves one page to the right
	Page Left	/J	Moves one page to the left
	Move Up	/M	Moves up one screen in the database
	Move Down	/V	Moves down one screen in the database
	Page Up	/G	Moves up one page
	Page Down	/W	Moves down one page
Help	About	/A	Tells you all about HanDBase

14 Forgot Valentine's Day Again: Gift Memo

Gift Memo, Version 1.1

giftmemo.webhostme.com

Commercial software: $10

Oops! Forget your honey's birthday? The boss's 45th anniversary of his par 4 performance? The kid's graduation present? Your dress size? Grandpa's hat size? Yikes! You need a life—and some help remembering, as well.

Gift Memo is a database (which means you need to install HanDBase to use it) that offers all the power of HanDBase, such as sorting and filtering data, and also comes with some predesigned databases that are very useful. These databases include

- ◆ The Birthstone Chart, which is a quick reference that can help when buying jewelry.

- ◆ The Dress Sizing Chart (sorry guys—nothing for you).

- ◆ The Child Sizing Chart, which lists relative ages, weights, and dimensions to make finding the correct size easier.

- ◆ The Shoe Conversion Chart to convert U.S. to European sizing for men and women. (Finally, you know what size your 44 Birkenstocks *really* are!).

- ◆ The Hat Sizing Chart based on head circumference (in inches or centimeters).

The commands for using Gift Memo are the same as for HanDBase.

15 Create Hierarchical Lists: BrainForest Mobile Edition

BrainForest Mobile Edition, Version 2.1

www.aportis.com

Shareware: $30

BrainForest helps you record, manage, and even generate everything from this week's shopping list (in categories, of course) to next year's plans for renting out the new condo to the dog's next scheduled bath. And what's especially useful and convenient is that you can edit a BrainForest file on either your Visor or your Windows machine; then, when you HotSync, the files on both machines are synchronized. (This means that when you update a file on one machine, it is also updated on the other machine at the same time.) In fact, you can export to any other desktop computer as long as you have software that supports the To Do or Memo format characteristic of the Visor application.

BrainForest accomplishes tracking of ideas and plans by creating what is known as a hierarchical tree (shown in the following graphic) where items can be prioritized, sorted, and arranged in any view that you find convenient. Trees consist of branches, which in turn consist of leaves (the smallest BrainForest unit). Items (such as a branch from one tree) can be dragged to another tree to become a branch or to another branch to become a leaf. In addition, notes can be attached anywhere along the way to add information to any entry.

BrainForest is an excellent tool for organizing material. It takes a bit of time to get used to this hierarchical arrangement, but once you do, it is easy to organize and move items around to meet your organizational needs.

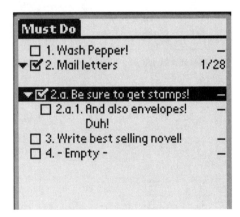

Getting Started with BrainForest

Follow these steps to create branches and leaves with BrainForest:

1. Tap the BrainForest icon to open the application.

2. Tap the Create button, or choose an already-created tree from the Tree Menu.

3. Enter the name of the new tree, and tap OK.

4. Tap New and enter information to be used in the tree.

5. Tap the check mark, or anywhere else, to complete your entry.

Check out the following table for a list of the commands you'll need to use BrainForest.

Menu	Command	Shortcut	What It Does
Tree	New Branch	/N	Creates a new branch on the tree
	New Leaf	/1	Creates a new leaf on the branch
	Delete Leaf/ Branch	/D	Deletes a leaf or a branch
	Details	/I	Sets the priority of a leaf and allows the specification of a start date
	Attach Note	/A	Attaches a note to a tree
	Delete Note	/O	Deletes a note attached to a tree and specifies if the item is done
	Purge	None	Purges all the branches and leaves that are done or finished
Edit	Cut Branch	/X	Removes a branch from a tree
	Copy Branch	/C	Copies a branch from one tree to another or to another part of the same tree
	Paste Branch	/P	Pastes a branch from one tree to another location on the same tree or to another tree

Menu	Command	Shortcut	What It Does
Edit	Copy Tree	None	Copies an entire tree
	Toggle Action	/T	Toggles between selecting an item or not
Show	Show/Hide	/-	Shows all items or only those that are date sensitive
	Arrange	None	Arranges the tree or branches by title in ascending or descending order
	Go To Next Undone	/	Goes to next item
	Go To Top	<	Goes to top of tree
	Go To Bottom	>	Goes to bottom of tree
	Expand All	/E	Expands all branches on a tree
	Collapse All	/Z	Collapses all branches of a tree
	Expand Branch	None	Expands a single branch
	Collapse Branch	None	Collapses a single branch
Options	Tree Preferences	None	Allows the user to set preferences such as new items being action items, show due dates, show numbering, and show priorities
	About BrainForest	None	Shares information about BrainForest, including how to order

16 Create To-Do Lists with Just a Tap of the Stylus: SuperList2

SuperList2, Version 2

`store.yahoo.com/pilotgearsw/tapsof.html`

Shareware: $12

Use your Visor's Memo Pad or To Do List to make a list of the stuff you need at the supermarket. Do either of those options come with more than 350 pre-entered grocery items? Do they allow you to create a simple list with nothing more than a tap of the stylus? Nope—and they're also not anywhere near as much fun as SuperList2. You can customize the Master List with new items (up to 20 characters), create a new list (for whomever might be doing the shopping), and enter up to 1,000 new items using Graffiti or the keyboard.

But why stop at creating a shopping list for the supermarket? You can create master lists for the hardware store and even sets of weekly tasks that are done on an intermittent basis. You can have up to 250 lists—that's a lot of Saturdays!

Getting Started with SuperList2

To use SuperList2, you need to load the following files:

- ◆ SuperList.prc (the SuperList program)
- ◆ AllItems.pdb
- ◆ AllLists.pdb

To create your own list, follow these steps:

1. Tap the item you want on the Master List (on the left side of the screen).

2. Tap the right side of the screen to add it to the list, and thereby create the current list.

3. To add your own item to be used in a later list, tap the Add button and enter the name of the item you want to add. SuperList2 will automatically save the list you create, and your list will be available the next time you open your application.

Want to search for bologna or spring water using SuperList2? Just enter the letters in the search field (unmarked but located in the lower-right corner of the Visor screen), and SuperList2 will take you there. To create more lists use the commands shown below.

Menu	Command	Shortcut	What It Does
Items	New	/N	Creates a new item for the Master List
	Delete	/D	Deletes an item from the Master List
	Edit	/E	Edits an item
	Clear	/L	Clears a list
	Grab All	/R	Copies all items in a list
	Select Item	/I	Selects an item
Lists	New	/W	Creates a new list

Menu	Command	Shortcut	What It Does
Lists	Delete	/H	Deletes a list
	Rename	/F	Renames a list
	Spawn	/Q	Copies a list based on another list
	Re-index	/Z	Re-indexes a list
Edit	Copy	/C	Copies an item
	Keyboard	/K	Enters information using the keyboard
	Graffiti Help	/G	Enters information using Graffiti
Options	Instructions	/T	Tells you how to use SuperList2
	Preferences	/B	Sets preferences for SuperList2
	About	/Y	Tells you all about SuperList2
	Register	/O	Registers SuperList2
	Register	None	Tells you how to register SuperList

Compute This!: a Calculator for Everything and Everyone

If you ever wanted to know the value of your Dell stock, how much Phil owes you for his share of the pizza (including the tip), or how to convert microns to millimeters, this section is for you. I will review some of the most interesting calculators available for your Visor, including PayUp!, PalmPilot, and SynCalc—all programs that make your life easier and your figuring more accurate.

17   Avoid Arguments over the Bill: PayUp!

PayUp! Version 1.1.1

www.portents.com

Shareware: $10

Jack owes $23.87, plus a 15 percent tip, Susan wants to pay only her share of the plate she split with Lois, and Lew is totally confused as to what he owes. PayUp! to the rescue. This is a full-featured restaurant-bill calculator that computes tax and gratuity and helps you divide the bill according to the cost of each person's meal. It will even compute change when someone (up to 19 people!) in the party overpays. No more arguments! Just good food and friends.

Cool features include tip and tax percentages and pull-down menus for the type of food ordered. You can use the keyboard or Graffiti to enter the ordered items. You can even edit the existing list of items or add new ones from your favorite restaurant and specify the type of currency, if it's not U.S. dollars. Every waiter should have a Visor and this program!

Want more? Check out these features:

◆ Manage orders for up to 19 diners

◆ Peruse pop-up menus that can include commonly ordered items

◆ Calculate change automatically for each diner

◆ Customize tax and tip rates

◆ Calculate the tip before or after tax

◆ Answer your questions using the tons of built-in help

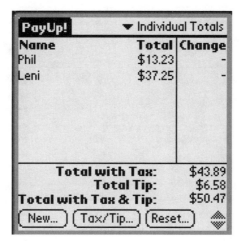

Getting Started with PayUp!

To use PayUp!, follow these steps:

1. Tap New to enter a new diner.

2. Enter the name of the diner.

3. Enter the name of the course (or choose from the list in the drop-down menu), and enter the amount the course costs, such as $7.95 for an appetizer.

4. Tap the Tax/Tip button.

5. Enter the tax and tip rates.

6. Tap OK.

Check out the table below for more cool commands.

Menu	Option	Shortcut	What It Does
Edit	Undo	/U	Undoes last operation
	Cut	/X	Cuts information
	Copy	/C	Copies information
	Paste	/P	Pastes information (ideal when two people order the same meal!)
	Keyboard	/K	Makes entries using the keyboard
	Graffiti	/G	Makes entries using Graffiti
Options	Preferences	/R	Specifies type of currency
	Help	/H	Presents one page of help
	About PayUp!	None	Tells you all about PayUp!
	Register PayUp!	None	Shows you how to register PayUp!

18 Convert Your Nautical Miles to Centimeters: PalmPilot Convertor Pro

PalmPilot Convertor Pro, Version 3

www.geocities.com/SiliconValley/Campus/7631/index.html

Shareware: $20

For the building contractor, pilot, potter, and even the butcher, baker, and candlestick maker, conversions count. PalmPilot Convertor Pro computes unit conversions by allowing you to select the unit you have from a drop-down list and convert it to another unit. You can choose between normal, scientific, and engineering notation. PalmPilot Convertor Pro is a simple Visor application—but one that is very useful.

More than 500 editable conversion factors are available within the 37 categories. Some of the conversion categories include the following:

◆ Length

◆ Illuminescence

◆ Power

◆ Mass

◆ Area

◆ Charge

◆ Density

◆ Volume

◆ Time

◆ Heat-flow rate

◆ Temperature

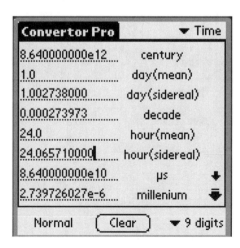

Getting Started with PalmPilot Convertor Pro

Follow these steps to use PalmPilot Convertor Pro:

1. Tap the PalmPilot Convertor Pro icon.

2. Choose the category of measures (length, area, etc.) you want to use.

3. Enter the value to be converted in the field corresponding to its measurement unit.

4. Tap the measurement unit name to perform conversions.

NOTE To see more results in different conversion units, scroll the list up or down by tapping the arrows. The larger arrows scroll five lines at a time.

The following table shows the important commands for PalmPilot Convertor Pro.

Menu	Option	Shortcut	What It Does
Option	Edit conversion factors	None	Allows you to edit the factors used in the conversion
Edit	Cut	/x	Cuts entries
	Copy	/c	Copies entries
	Paste	/p	Pastes entries
Help	About	/a	Tells you all about PalmPilot Convert

19 Perform Complex Mathematical Operations: SynCalc Demo

SynCalc Demo, Version 1.5

info@synsolutions.com/software/syncalc

Commercial software: $17.95

If you need to add up the cost of your groceries, the Visor calculator will do just fine. Anything more complex? Try SynCalc, the mother of all calculators. Not only can it do regular and unimaginative calculations, such as 2 + 2, but it also allows the user to execute complex calculations using an unlimited number of nested parentheses and functions. You can choose between normal, fixed, scientific, and hexadecimal formats; record the most recent calculations with a printer tape; and drag and drop just about anywhere. And as if that's not enough, SynCalc remembers 12 memory locations (which means you can enter 12 recently used values and never have to re-enter them) and includes as extensive a set of manuals as you are likely to find for any Visor application.

Are there other wonderful features? Try these:

◆ Definition of 100 user-defined shortcuts

◆ Real-time input and output functions

◆ Drag-and-drop from any large button that can hold a text expression

◆ Double- and triple-tap editing

◆ Twelve memory locations that are drag-and-drop accessible

◆ Macro support (a great time-saver)

◆ Algebraic parsing of expressions

◆ Nested parentheses and functions

◆ Full drag-and-drop functionality

◆ MathPlugin: trig, log, and other basic math functions

◆ BaseConvertor: Hex, Octal, and Binary convertors

◆ LogicPlugin: if() and iftext() functions for conditional results

◆ Up to 100 easily programmable macros (SynCalc's Shortcuts) that make quick work of tough calculations

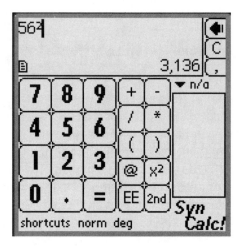

This table shows the important commands you'll use in this program.

Menu	Option	Shortcut	What It Does
Calc	View Memory	/V	Views the values assigned to the Visor buttons and text letters
	View Calculation Log	/L	Views the log of calculations that have already been completed
	View Console	/M	Views output
	Edit Shortcuts	/O	Edits the built-in shortcuts (or you can create your own)

Menu	Option	Shortcut	What It Does
Calc	Function Browser	/F	Examines functions
	SynCalc Tour	/T	Allows you to take a tour
	How To Order SynCalc	None	Shows you how to order SynCalc
Edit	Undo	/U	Undoes last operation
	Cut	/X	Cuts information
	Copy	/C	Copies information
	Paste	/P	Pastes information
	Select All	/S	Selects all calculations
	Keyboard	/K	Uses the keyboard to enter data
	Graffiti	/G	Uses Graffiti to enter data
	Ans > Clipboard	/A	Sends the calculation to the clipboard for pasting later or for creating a memory entry
Options	About SynCalc	None	Tells you all about SynCalc
	Preferences	/R	Defines size of screen font for answer and display, thousands separator, and whether you want the expression area cleared on start-up
	Import Shortcuts	/I	Imports shortcuts to other applications
	Export Shortcuts	/E	Exports shortcuts from other applications

20 Calculate How Much You Owe: LoanPayment

LoanPayment, Version 2.01U

members.aol.com/ekstrandbb

Shareware: $10.00

Okay, so your boat hasn't come in yet, but it's still a good idea to take a look at your interest rate on the car, houseboat, and credit card loan and take a shot at what it "could be." That's what LoanPayment does for you with little trouble and lots of accuracy.

So why another loan calculator? Here's why: LoanPayment allows the user to

◆ Enter the loan amount, the number of payments per year, the number of years the loan is for, and the yearly interest rate to figure out your payment.

◆ Calculate early payoff and interest saved.

◆ Calculate an alternate payment schedule.

◆ Calculate the maximum affordable loan.

◆ Calculate interest rate.

◆ Save any calculation to the Palm Memo Pad.

NOTE The coolest thing about this software is that it's Char-Ware—all the proceeds from registration go to the Juvenile Diabetes Foundation! This is a generous gesture on the part of the developer. Anyone at Microsoft or IBM or Dell reading this?

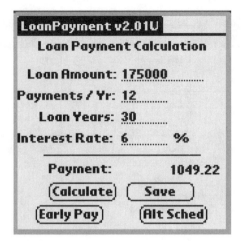

Getting Started with LoanPayment

Here's how to find out exactly how much you'll save with that lower interest rate.

1. Enter the loan amount.

2. Enter the number of payments per year.

3. Enter the number of years on the loan.

4. Enter the interest rate (remember that it's a percent).

5. Tap Calculate, and see the new payment.

NOTE You can use the Options menu to compute other values, such as the maximum loan you can afford or the interest rate given other loan information.

The following table shows the important commands for LoanPayment.

Menu	Command	Shortcut	What It Does
Edit	Undo	/U	Undoes most recent operation
	Cut	/C	Removes information
	Copy	/X	Copies information
	Paste	/P	Pastes information
	Keyboard	/K	Uses the keyboard to enter information
	Graffiti	/G	Uses Graffiti to enter information
Options	Loan Payment	None	Computes the loan payment
	Maximum Amount	/R	Computes the maximum amount of a loan
	Interest Calc	/H	Computes the interest rate
Info	About LoanPayment	None	Tells you about LoanPayment
	About Char-Ware	None	Tells you about Charity Ware
	About Diabetes	None	Discusses diabetes
	Register	None	Tells you how to register LoanPayment

It's Your Business!

When was the last time you *didn't* see someone with a cell phone appearing as if the deal of a lifetime is about to be made? With all this new cellular technology, everything's going mobile ; especially business transactions. Your Visor can help you do everything (and even check on your stock portfolio—see Stock Manager) from computing the best rates for a lease, checking on how your eBay stock is doing, or keeping your desktop Quicken data at your fingertips while you're in the back of a taxi. As the Visor becomes more popular, and it supports more and more business applications, you'll see the Visor and new ideas regularly springing up in Dilbert's cubicle next to you.

21 Trade Stocks from Your Visor: Touchwise

Touchwise, Version 1

www.touchwise.com

Freeware

Many of the applications that we are featuring in *Visor! I Didn't Know You Could Do That* are very simple to install, configure, and use. However, some are a bit more difficult (and some take a good deal of tenacity to get going, like Touchwise), but the results are more than worth it. Touchwise is one such application that allows trading of stocks, options, bonds, and mutual funds over your Visor OS device's network connection. You can have access to all of your brokerage account information—as well as real-time quotes—and sell or buy data using a wireless IP modem (such as those offered by Handspring). The installation process is long, but as you will see, the work can well be worth it when it comes time to find out just how well your eBay stock has done.

Getting Started with Touchwise

Configuring Touchwise is where all the work is. Our example here is with the Minstrel Wireless modem because it's the most widely used in the PalmPilot (but other modems work the same way with the Visor). Here's how to do it:

1. Select the Network category from the Prefs application.

2. Type in a new name for the network setup, which in this case would be Minstrel.

3. Tap the phone number field and enter **00**. Be sure to leave the user-name and password fields blank.

4. Tap the Details button, enter the appropriate DNS and IP Address settings (you can get these from your wireless service provider), and set the properties as follows:

   Connection type PPP

   Idle timeout Power Off

5. Tap the Script button and enter in the following script (the settings you enter appear in bold):

   ◆ Delay: **1**

   ◆ Send: **at\appp**

   ◆ Send CR: (leave this field blank)

   ◆ Wait For: **1**

   ◆ End:

6. Tap the OK button.

7. Tap the Connect button. You will see a message telling you that a connection has been established.

8. Launch the Touchwise application from the main application screen. The top-right button enclosing just a "." (dot) will connect you to the Touchwise trading server with a demo username and password.

9. Enter a stock or option symbol and you should see the delayed quote.

22 Keep Track of Your Money: FCPlus Professional

FCPlus Professional, Version 2

www.infinitysw.com

Commercial software: $39.95

Want to know how much that lease will be? The value of your Dell stock? How big will the payments be on that Cadillac Escade? Then check out FCPlus Professional. It's a business calculator that allows you to compute any of the following:

◆ Annuities

◆ Loans and leases

- The time value of money

- Amortization

- Complex and simple interest

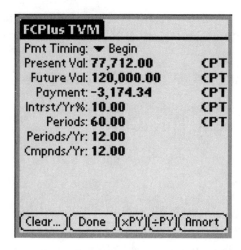

Also included with the software are features that allow you to calculate markups and markdowns, profit margin, and percent changes (great for retailers). The mathematical functions that are offered include power, square root, reciprocal, natural log, square, exponential, and factorial. FCPlus Professional works in both RPN (*reverse polish notation*) for ease of data entry and calculations, and standard input modes. Ten memory locations allow you to insert recorded data anywhere within the application—you can even cut and paste the price of that new car right into the contract (which, of course, you already have on your Visor). Perhaps the most appealing feature of this Visor application is that, unlike other calculators, it goes way beyond data entry and provides worksheets for individual applications.

The new version comes with loads of improvements and new features, such as:

- More intuitive worksheet designs

- Bond computations

- Currency conversions

- Unit conversions, including area, mass, length, volume, and temperature

- ◆ Cash-flow computations including net present value, internal rate of return, and net

- ◆ Future value, modified internal rate of return, net uniform series, payback, and profitability index

- ◆ Statistics, depreciation, interest conversion, and simple interest computations

Getting Started with FCPlus Professional

Here's how to compute the Time Value of Money, which is the only working module available in the demo:

1. On the opening screen, click WKST (for worksheet).

2. Scroll and tap on TVM (for Time Value of Money).

3. Tap the Present Value button and use the keypad to enter the present value of the money.

4. Continue to enter values by repeating step 3.

5. Tap the value to the right of the Payment button to see what the value of the payment needs to be.

There are many, many commands for FCPlus Professional, depending upon which screen you are using. The most basic (and all that you need to get stated) are shown here.

Menu	Option	Shortcut	What It Does
Options	About FCPlus Professional	None	About FCPlus Professional
	Preferences	/R	Sets decimal places

23 Calculate the Costs: Lease-It!

Lease-It! Version 2

`www.pe.net/firm/dpw-designs/`

Shareware: $10

It seems like nobody is buying anything these days. Cars, computers, and even the TV are just leased until a new version or model comes out in a few months. If you want to figure out the costs associated with leasing, Lease-It! does a good job with minimum effort on your part. You just need to input the critical variables and Lease-It! will help to take the mystery out of leasing by showing you exactly where your money is going and how it is being spent.

Lease-It! can help you solve for

- ◆ Capitalized cost
- ◆ Capitalized cost reduction
- ◆ Term
- ◆ Interest rate/money factor
- ◆ Monthly payment

You can also perform sophisticated "what if" calculations to arrive at a desired monthly payment by varying the input numbers, such as cost and residual value (what it's worth when the lease is over). That way you can work with the numbers until a payment that fits your needs can be found.

```
┌─────────────────────────────────────────┐
│ Lease-It! ▼ Monthly Payment             │
│ » Volvo                                  │
│                    MSRP: $   34,000      │
│         Capitalized Cost: $   30,000     │
│      Cap. Cost Reduction: $      0       │
│      ▼ Residual Value: $      0          │
│                    Term:         48 mos  │
│        ▼ Money Factor:        0          │
│                    Base: $   625.00      │
│                   Taxes: $      0        │
│         Monthly Payment: $   625.00      │
│ ( Done )                                 │
└─────────────────────────────────────────┘
```

Getting Started with Lease-It!

Follow along with these steps to get started with Lease-It!:

1. Tap New.

2. Enter a name for the item you will be calculating information for (such as house, Volvo, college education).

3. At the top of the main form, select from the a pop-up list the variable you want to solve for, including any of the following:

◆ Capitalized cost

◆ Capital cost reduction

◆ Term

◆ Interest rate or money factor

◆ Monthly payment

4. Complete the blank fields.

Lease-It! has a number of commands, shown in the following table.

Menu	Command	Shortcut	What It Does
Commands	Erase	/E	Clears all of the fields on the form.
	Delete Record	/D	Deletes a record.
	Register...	/R	Displays the registration information screen. This screen is displayed only if the application has not been registered.
Edit	Undo	/U	Undoes the last operation.
	Cut	/X	Removes highlighted text and copies it to the clipboard.
	Copy	/C	Copies highlighted text to the Clipboard.
	Paste	/P	Pastes text from the Clipboard.
	Keyboard	/K	Uses the keyboard to enter information.
Options	Taxes	None	Provides information and calculations about tax options.
	About Lease-It!	None	All about Lease-It!.

24 Let Visor Manage Your Finances: QMate

Qmate, Version 1.52

`www.qmate.com`

Shareware: $20

If you like Quicken, the most popular, personal financial-management software in the galaxy, then you will love QMate, which comes in both a Windows and Mac version. Not only can you track simple financial operations, such as checkbook entries and balances, but QMate is sophisticated and smart enough to allow you to do the following:

◆ Use memorized transactions, called *QuickFill* (a Quicken feature that saves you time), for payee and category fields

◆ Auto-increment date and number fields

◆ Split transactions

◆ Security via password protection

◆ Transfer funds between accounts

◆ Maintain up to 32 accounts

◆ Convert currencies with conversion rates

◆ Use sorting options for selecting and showing only the transactions you want to see

◆ Integrate with the popular budgeting application QuikBudget

NOTE Together, QMate and QuikBudget offer a very powerful solution to your financial tracking needs.

QMate is also compatible with Microsoft Money and offers an extensive and clearly written Internet-based manual that contains basic and advanced instructions as well as FAQs to get you started. This is one of those Visor applications that closely matches its PC and Mac counterpart and is simple to use but has great deal of features.

Finally, if you become a real Qmate power user, consider using Qmate-Entry, which creates a new transaction and navigates to the New Transaction dialog box in the account you last used in QMate.

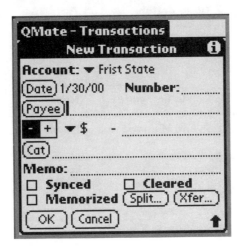

Getting Started with QMate

To create a new account, follow these steps:

1. Tap the New button on the Accounts form.

2. Specify the account name using up to 32 characters, the account type, and the default currency and balance.

3. Tap the Transactions button.

Follow these steps to enter a transaction:

1. Tap the New button on the New Transaction form.

2. Enter the appropriate information, such as Date, Number, Payee, Amount, etc.

3. Click OK.

This table displays QMate's commands and shortcuts.

Menu	Option	Shortcut	What It Does
List	Go to Top	/T	Goes to the top of a list
	Go to Bottom	/B	Goes to the bottom of a list
	Edit Currencies	/R	Edits your list of currencies
	Delete Categories	None	Deletes a category
	Delete Memorized	None	Deletes a memorized transaction
Edit	Cut	/X	Cuts information
	Copy	/C	Copies information
	Paste	/P	Pastes information
	Undo	/U	Undoes the last operation
	Select All	/S	Selects all the information in a transaction
	Keyboard	/K	Uses the keyboard to enter information
	Graffiti	/G	Uses Graffiti to enter information
Options	Preferences	None	Sets preferences such as date default and location of currency symbol
	Purge	/D	Purges a transaction or set of transactions based on dates
	Synced/Cleared Status	/Y	Finds the status of your latest HotSync

Menu	Option	Shortcut	What It Does
Options	Set Password	None	Sets a password and defines a hint to help you remember
	About QMate	/I	All about QMate

25 Keep Yourself in Line: QuikBudget

QuikBudget 2.6 Millennium

www.QuikBudget.com

Shareware: $19.95

It seems like every generation of shareware gets better—including Quik-Budget. This program is a well-designed and powerful tool for keeping track of your "ins" and "outs," or rather, your expenses that change every month. QuikBudget lets you create numerous "wallets" to track the flow of bucks in and out of a particular category. You indicate how much to add to the wallet, and it will do it for you every week, every two weeks, every half-month, or every month (just like payday). And to start, QuikBudget has already set up wallets for Dining, Entertainment, Groceries, and House-hold transactions as you'll see in the graphic. If you really want to stick to a budget, this is the way to do it.

Other notable features include

◆ Independent subwallets

◆ Compatibility with Excel

◆ Automatic sales tax pop-up list

◆ Access to foreign currencies

- ◆ Noncumulative wallets (so more than one Visor user can use the same version of QuickMate)
- ◆ Wallet merging (great for adding together categories after you realize they could have been together in the first place)
- ◆ Easy filtering of transactions
- ◆ Favorite wallets (the ones you use most often)
- ◆ Quick and Edit modes
- ◆ Password protection
- ◆ Semimonthly and monthly payday support
- ◆ Adjustable number field width
- ◆ Thousands separators

In addition, Quik Budget adds auto-fill to the expense summary form, improves the Preferences and Show forms, and distinguishes between automatic and manual transfers.

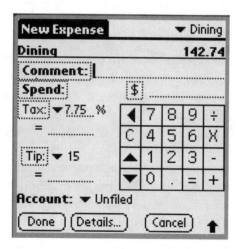

Getting Started with QuikBudget

To start a new transaction, follow these steps:

1. Tap the New button.

2. Specify a name for the Wallet.

3. Enter an amount for this specific time period.

4. Enter the amount remaining in this period (usually $0 if a new wallet and time period).

5. Tap OK.

Follow these steps to enter a transaction:

1. From the opening screen, tap on the wallet you want to use.

2. Add any comment you might have on the transaction by tapping the New button and entering text in the Comment area.

3. Enter the amount of the purchase or the activity on which money was spent by using the onscreen keypad.

4. Tap Done.

This table should get you familiar with QuikBudget.

Menu	Command	Shortcut	What It Does
Wallet	Delete Wallet	/D	Deletes a wallet
	Edit Wallet	/E	Edits an existing wallet
	Purge All Wallets	/W	Deletes all wallets
Edit	Undo	/U	Undoes the last operation
	Copy	/X	Copies information from QuickMate to the Visor Clipboard

Menu	Command	Shortcut	What It Does
Edit	Cut	/C	Removes information from QuickMate and places it in the Visor clipboard
	Paste	/P	Pastes information from the Clipboard into a designated area
	Select All	/S	Selects all the data in a wallet
	Keyboard	/K	Uses the keyboard to enter data
	Graffiti	/G	Uses Graffiti to enter data
Options	Preferences	/R	Sets whether a specific type of calculation is used, whether there is a tip on taxes, and what the home currency is
	Security	/Y	Allows you to hide records and set password characteristics
	Define Currencies/ Countries	None	Specifies current currency
	Payday	None	Lets you enter how often you get paid (weekly, semiweekly, etc.) and when (specifying the date)
	Register	None	Allows you to register
	About QuikBudget	none	All about QuikBudget

26 Create Spreadsheets: Quicksheet

Quicksheet, Version 4.1

www.cesinc.com/index.html

Commercial software: $49.95

Anyone who deals with information needs a *spreadsheet,* an electronic ledger of rows and columns. Quicksheet is a fully functional tool that allows you all the functions of a spreadsheet. Much like Excel, you can synchronize the files as well as access your Visor spreadsheets. Quicksheet *is* the mother of all spreadsheets. Quicksheet's features include:

- ◆ A striking similarity to the real spreadsheet on your desktop so you can get started immediately

- ◆ 48 built-in scientific, financial, statistical, date and time, lookup, and aggregate functions

- ◆ Support of multiple sheets per workbook and the ability to link the sheets

- ◆ 996 rows × 254 columns per sheet (B-I-G!)

- ◆ The formatting of cells in a number of different ways and the ability to name the styles available for use with the open spreadsheet

- ◆ Support of row and column freezing, column resizing, and cell locking with sheet

- ◆ Search and replace values and formulas

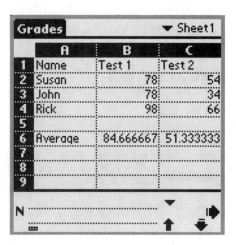

Getting Started with Quicksheet

To create a sample worksheet, follow these steps:

1. Tap the New icon.

2. Enter a name for the worksheet, and tap OK.

3. In cell A1, enter **Rent**.

4. In cell A2, enter **Food**.

5. In cell A3, enter **Car**.

6. In cell B1, enter **$300**.

7. In cell B2, enter **$50**.

8. In cell B3, enter **$28**.

9. In cell B4, enter **SUM(b1,b3)**, which sums the scores from cell B1 through B3.

10. Click any other cell and you'll see the sum in cell B4.

Check out the following table for Quicksheet's commands.

Menu	Command	Shortcut	What It Does
Book	**About Quicksheet**	**None**	**All about Quicksheet**
	Help	**/H**	**Help**
	Save	**/S**	**Saves a worksheet**
	Save As	**/A**	**Saves a worksheet under a new name**
	Properties	**/O**	**Examines the properties of a worksheet, including appearance and backup options**
	Recalc Now	**/N**	**Recomputes formula values**
	Protect	**/+**	**Protects a worksheet from changes**
	Unprotect	**/-**	**Unprotects a worksheet**
	Close	**/E**	**Closes a worksheet**
Edit	**Undo**	**/U**	**Undoes the last operation**
	Cut	**/X**	**Cuts data**
	Copy	**/C**	**Copies data**
	Paste	**/P**	**Pastes data**
	Paste Special	**/V**	**Pastes data from another application or formula**
	Formatting	**/M**	**Formats cells**
	Clear	**/***	**Clears cells**

Menu	Command	Shortcut	What It Does
Edit	Select All	/I/	Selects the entire worksheet
	Extend Selection	/J	Extends the selection of cells
	Keyboard	/K	Enters data using the keyboard
	Graffiti	/G	Enters data using graffiti
Page	Top	/T	Goes to he top of the page
	Bottom	/B	Goes to the bottom of the page
	Up	/Y	Moves up one cell
	Down	/D	Moves down one cell
	Left	/W	Moves left once cell
	Right	/Z	Moves right one cell

27 Registering on Your Visor: MyCheckbook

MyCheckbook, Version 2

http://www.palmpage.com/quickster/

Freeware

Sometimes simple is best. MyCheckbook is your good ol' basic register that records and tracks your checkbook activity. It has the following special features:

◆ Displays checkbook register (7 transactions) on main form

◆ Scrolls register up or down one line or one page at a time

◆ Changes the date for any transaction before you save it

◆ Assigns a check/transaction to a particular category

◆ Reconciles checkbook register from the main form

◆ Exports the checkbook register to the MemoPad

Getting Started with MyCheckbook

To start an account in MyCheckbook, follow these steps:

1. Tap the New button and select the type of transaction from the drop-down menu.

2. Enter a title for the transaction in the To field.

3. Enter the amount of the transaction.

4. Tap Enter.

About Those Buttons

MyCheckbook contains four buttons. The following list tells you what these buttons are and what they are used for:

The New button Presents a drop-down list that allows you to select a transaction type, including

◆ Next number (gets the next check number)

◆ New number (enters a new check number)

◆ ATM

◆ Swiped (for use when using a debit card)

◆ Transfer (when you transfer money from your checking account)

◆ Deposit (when you make a deposit)

The Enter button Completes all transactions.

The Cancel button Cancels a transaction.

The Details button Allows you to group, assign, or check into different categories. If you wish to edit the categories, select the Edit Categories option from the pop-up list.

The commands for MyCheckbook are relatively simple, as in this table.

Menu	Command	What It Does
Options	Reconcile	Helps you reconcile the bank statement and your checkbook activity
	Preferences	Allows you to set display options
	Export Register	Exports a Register to the Visor MemoPad
	Number of Records	Shows the number of records
	About MyCheckbook	All about MyCheckbook

28 Keep Tabs on Who Owes What: IOUMate

IOUMate, Version 1

`www.palmmate.com/ioumate/index.html`

Freeware

Never a lender nor a borrower be! In my quest to provide you with only the most useful Visor applications, I bring you IOUMate. Ever lose that book to a friend? Forget what John and Ann owe you? Remember that you gave away Kristen Baki's *Lives of the Monster Dogs* in its first edition, but you have no idea where it is now? Don't fret. IOUMate is like a well-designed, dedicated database that keeps a record of to whom you lent what. Here are just some of the things that IOUMate features:

- ◆ All entries are presented in a table format containing the name, item description, and amount owed.

- ◆ You can sort the table by any column by simply tapping the column's title.

- ◆ You can edit existing and create new categories (such as Goodies!).

- ◆ You can change sort order (up/down) by again tapping a column title.

- ◆ You can resize columns just like in any desktop application.

- ◆ You can view entries by any category, whether it's a person or an item, with an enhanced category mechanism.

◆ You can track what others owe you and you owe others by tapping the little stick figure.

Getting Started with IOUMate

To create an entry in IOUMate, follow these steps:

1. Open the application on your Visor.

2. Tap the New button.

3. Enter a name of the item, use the pull-down menu (▼) to select the name of an individual, or use the Edit option to create a new name.

4. Enter a description of the item.

5. Enter the amount of money (or other item) owed.

6. Click OK.

This table lists the commands for IOUMate.

Menu	Command	Shortcut	What It Does
Record	New Record	/N	Creates a new record
Edit	Undo	/U	Undoes the last operation

Menu	Command	Shortcut	What It Does
Edit	Cut	/X	Cuts an entry
	Copy	/C	Copies an entry
	Paste	/P	Pastes an entry
	Select All	/A	Selects all entries
	Keyboard	/K	Uses the keyboard to enter information
	Graffiti	/C	Uses Graffiti to enter information
Options	About IOUMate		All about IOUMate
	Preferences	/R	Sets IOUMate to remember last category or not
	Help	/H	Help
	How to Register		Registration directions
	Registration Code		Enters the registration code you received via e-mail

29 Don't Over Stamp: PostCalc

PostCalc, Version 1

www.dovcom.com/pilot/postcalc.html

Shareware: $10

You still have to lick the stamp and put it on that letter, but PostCalc will help you determine how many stamps. From one-half ounce to 12 ounces, PostCalc will tell you the air and surface postal costs for a particular destination and weight, automatically computed in U.S. postage costs. And if you made it to the Millennium, the postage rates are all current (but don't hold your breath—a rate rise is coming).

```
┌──────────────────────────────────────────┐
│ PostCalc (UNREGISTERED)                   │
│ Weight (oz)   Destination                 │
│ ┌──────┐   ┌──────────────┐               │
│ │ 0.5  │   │ United States │               │
│ │ 1.0  │   │ Canada        │               │
│ │ 1.5  │   │ Mexico        │               │
│ │ 2.0  │   │ Other Country │               │
│ │ 2.5  │   └──────────────┘               │
│ │ 3.0  │                                   │
│ │ 3.5  │        Air: $0.99 ........        │
│ │ 4.0  │                                   │
│ │ 4.5  │        Surface: N/A ........      │
│ │ 5.0  │                                   │
│ │ 5.5 ↓│                                   │
│ └──────┘                                   │
└──────────────────────────────────────────┘
```

Getting Started with PostCalc

To use PostCalc, follow these steps:

1. From the drop-down menu, select the weight of what you want to send.

2. Click the country you are sending to, and then choose the country you are sending from (the United States, Canada, Mexico, or Other).

3. Read the Air and Surface charges.

There are just a couple of commands that you need to know for PostCalc, and they are shown in this table.

Menu	Command	Shortcut	What It Does
Options	About PostCalc	/A	All about PostCalc
	How to Register	/H	How to register PostCalc

30 Buy Low and Sell High: Stock Manager

Stock Manager

`PalmStocks.net/default.htm`

Shareware: $19.95

With discount brokers going crazy (and lowering commissions), you can be even more in charge of your portfolio with programs like StockBroker, where you can easily connect to your network and download all your current stock prices. You need a connection to the Internet, such as through a modem snapped on to your Visor (or the wireless thing that is sure to come along for the Visor at any time), and you're set.

Don't be concerned if you're a global investor. The following stock exchanges are supported: NYSE and NASDAQ in the U.S.; the Montreal, Vancouver, and Alberta in Canada; Barcelona, Berlin, Bilbao, Bremen, Copenhagen, Dusseldorf, Frankfurt, Hamburg, Hanover, London, Madrid, Madrid CE, Milan, Munich, Oslo, Paris, Stockholm, Stuttgart, Valencia, and Xetra exchanges in Europe, and almost any other one you're smart enough to invest in.

Some outstanding features include:

◆ Working with names or symbols

◆ Computing rate of stock value change or dividend

◆ Showing profit as a percent, change in value, change in percent, and several other indicators

The main screen shows all your stocks in the currently selected portfolio. You can tap the first, second, or third column header to change what is displayed in that column. The fourth column shows whether the stock has gone up or down since the last Internet update, and tapping this icon brings up the market window for the corresponding stock. The fifth column shows whether a particular stock has a note attached to it, and you can tap this column to open an existing note or to create a new note for the corresponding stock.

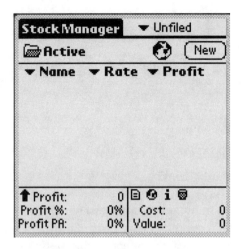

Getting Started with Stock Manager

Stock Manager does lots, but the one thing you always want to know is how much money you've made (or lost). Here's how:

1. Tap the Stock Manager icon.

2. Tap the big globe icon. Stock Manager connects and you will shortly see your profits (or losses).

Stock Manager has a bunch of commands that fit the complexity of what it can do (as shown below)

Menu	Command	Shortcut	What It Does
Record	New Stocks	/N	Enters a new stock
	Stock Details	/I	Shows the details of a stock
	Delete Stock	/D	Deletes a stock
	Split Stock	None	Records a stock split
	Sort Stocks	/S	Sorts stocks

Menu	Command	Shortcut	What It Does
Record	Preferences	None	Sets preferences for Stock Manager
Edit	Cut	/C	Removes information
	Copy	/X	Copies information
	Paste	/P	Pastes information
	Select All	/A	Selects all information
	Keyboard	/K	Uses the keyboard to enter information
	Graffiti	/G	Uses Graffiti to enter information
Network	Update Stocks	/U	Updates your stock prices
	View Log	/V	Views past transactions
	Network Panel	/T	Defines service settings
	Modem Panel	/M	Works with your modem settings
	Network Settings	/B	Works with your network settings
Help	About	/A	About Stock Broker
	Register	None	Registers Stock Broker
	Show HotSync ID	None	Shows HotSync ID

31 Create a Safe Visor: OnlyMe

OnlyMe, Version 1.9

www.tranzoa.com/html/tranzoa.htm

Shareware: $9.95

Businesses need secrecy and security, and you can have both through OnlyMe, which can automatically lock your Visor whenever you turn it off. This program is a quick, easy, and secure way to protect sensitive information. OnlyMe locks your Visor whenever the screen is turned off, and that's all you need to do to ensure the privacy of your information. In addition, entering your OnlyMe password is as easy as one stroke of the stylus or finger, and your Visor will return to where it was when you last signed off.

WARNING This is not an application that is to be taken lightly. It works very well, and you should only use it if you are very interested in preventing anyone from accessing your Visor. The ONLYME.HTM file that comes with the software should be read before the program is installed.

Getting Started with OnlyMe

OnlyMe is simple to use, but you have to remember one thing—your password. And don't try storing it on your Visor (duh!). To enter a password, do the following:

1. Tap the OnlyMe icon.

2. Tap the Set password button.

3. Enter the set of codes you want to use.

4. Confirm the password.

5. If you want to use OnlyMe, then click the Enable OnlyMe box.

The next time you start your Visor, you'll see a set of buttons, of which a certain combination (determined by you) constitutes the passwords from which you can choose.

You can also use the buttons on your Visor to enter the password (since the on-screen and the real Visor buttons are positioned alike). So, there are four ways to enter your password:

◆ OnlyMe on-screen Buttons

◆ Graffiti letters

◆ Graffiti digits

◆ Hardware buttons

If you're worried about someone guessing your password, don't be. If you use only five buttons, we're still talking about more than 9,000 possibilities. Good luck.

The table that follows shows the commands for OnlyMe.

Menu	Command	Shortcut	What It Does
Operations	Reset History	/R	Reviews password settings
Help	Information	/I	Lots of information about how to use OnlyMe
	About OnlyMe	/A	About OnlyMe

32 The Best Way to Decide Your Next Step: Pocket Pareto

Pocket Pareto, Version 1

amsoftw.tripod.com/ppareto.htm

Shareware: $5.00

You're a busy bee, with work, school, family, and other responsibilities. Wouldn't it be nice to have a tool that can help you make some general decisions about what to do when? Pocket Pareto is a simple yet useful tool. You enter the name of the thing to do, the relative value you (or your boss) places on it, and the relative amount of time. (We say relative because you're comparing these different "to do's" to one another.) You can enter up to seven tasks that you need prioritized.

Then it's a simple tap on the Calculate button, and you see which tasks should be done more, which tasks less, and which have about the same value.

```
┌─────────────────────────────────┐
│ PocketPareto                    │
├─────────────────────────────────┤
│ Do More:  pick up clothes        │
│ Same:     final report           │
│           personal biz           │
│           Pooch to vet           │
│ Do Less:  agent calls            │
│                                  │
│                                  │
│                                  │
│            ( Return )            │
└─────────────────────────────────┘
```

Getting Started with Pocket Pareto

To use Pocket Pareto, follow these steps:

1. Tap the Pocket Pareto icon.

2. Enter the name of the item to task.

3. Using the drop-down arrow, tap the relative priority (from 1 to 7) of the task.

4. Using the drop-down arrow, tap the relative amount of time the task will take.

5. Tap Calculate.

33 Liven Up Your Dull Speech: Palm Quotes

Palm Quotes, Version 1.1

Not Avaliable

Freeware

How's this?

> "Sex without love is an empty experience, but as empty experiences go it's one of the best."
>
> —Woody Allen

It's your turn to make the big speech, and believe it or not, you've forgotten your notes. But you haven't left home without your Visor, and with it, you know you can have more than 500 quotes, quips, jokes, and jingles that can at least keep the audience entertained until it's time for the next course in your chicken à la king dinner.

Palm Quotes is a collection of quotes and other goodies (100 on the demo and 500 on the real thing) that can keep people entertained, distracted, or whatever you need to do with words and an attentive audience. You can jump to different quotes, see them at random, by author, by keyword, and by category. Some categories include:

- Aging
- Business
- Celebrities
- Classic
- Crime
- Death
- Education
- Ethics
- Failure
- God
- Happiness
- Humor
- Ideas
- Knowledge
- Leadership
- Life
- Literature
- Love
- Sex

In addition, categories can be combined, such as Humor *and* Life. Palm Quotes looks deceptively simple but contains lots of fun words and can be very useful.

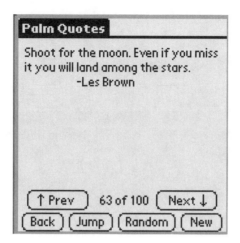

Getting Started with Palm Quotes

To use Palm Quotes, follow these steps:

1. Tap the Quotes icon.

2. Select between Category, Keyword, or Author, or click the Random Quote button, the List All Quotes button, or Program Info.

3. Double-click the first line of the quote to see the entire quote.

Keeping Time: Clocks and Calendars

There's only one thing you can't make more of, and that's time. But by using these various Visor applications, you can certainly learn how to keep track of it in a variety of different ways. And while you're at it, you can keep track of your appointments as well.

So, when you're off to accept the company's employee-of-the-month award and only have 45 seconds for your speech, try BigClock to help you track the time and then Action Names to see who your next appointment is with. And never, ever forget your honey's (choose one: birthday, anniversary, plastic surgery operation) by keeping DateMate close by.

34 Use Split Screen When Reviewing Your Appointments: Action Names

Action Names, Version 4.4

www.iambic.com/pilot/actionnames/downloadfile.htm

Shareware: $19.95

Instead of having to tap away to see all the information about any appointment you have, Action Names (kind of like your Visor Date Book on steroids) allows you to see all the information about an appointment—such as related phone calls or meetings—in a single split screen. You can see your schedule for the day, week, month, quarter, and even split days and view the separate sections. No more crazed tapping to see if what you have to do can be done on a certain day and at a certain time. An alarm—including a snooze button—can be set for each event in case you forget to look at your Visor.

Some of the new features include

◆ Week Grid view now shows overdue ToDo's from previous weeks listed on today's date.

◆ Added an "Options" menu to the Address Edit view, which allows you to select your font.

◆ Added a preference for the Split Agenda view to show only scheduled time.

◆ You can now group by ZIP code in Contact view.

Getting Started with Action Names

Follow these steps to get started with Action Names:

1. Tap the time you want to enter a new appointment.

2. Enter the name of the contact (or whom the appointment is with).

3. Set the duration of the appointment.

4. Enter any description.

5. Tap OK.

The following table will get you familiar with the Action Names commands and shortcuts.

Menu	Option	Shortcut	What It Does
New	New Meeting	/M	Schedules a new meeting
	New Call	/Z	Schedules a new call
	New ToDo	/T	Schedules a new item for the ToDo list
Options	Preferences	/R	Sets the preferences for an appointment or call
	Display Options	/Y	Sets options for displaying appointments and calls
	Purge	/E	Purges events based on dates
	Edit Icons	/V	Allows you to customize icons
	About Action Names	None	Tells you about Action Names

35 Turn Your Visor into a Giant Clock: BigClock

BigClock, Version 2.51

www.gacel.de

Freeware

This is the perfect clock for anyone who needs a really B-I-G display (and that's not just those of us who have weak eyes). It's great for timing yourself when giving talks or teaching (just a glance will do) or any other situation where you have to know the time, keep time, or time something. Not only do you get the date and time in a large format, but the alarm function allows for up to four alarms, with four different alarm sounds to accompany your wake-up call or time-to-get-the-kids call. If the noise is too much, try the silent alarm or the backlight alarm (the flashing is cool), or snooze so you can roll over for a few more minutes. Other timely features include the following:

- The world option shows the local time as well as the time in four other locations.
- The timer screen displays a stopwatch that can count up or down.
- Numbers are displayed in very large letters.
- You can use up to four alarms.
- You can use up to four timers/counters.
- There are four configurable sounds.
- Want some extra z-z-z-z's—use the snooze alarm.
- Use up to eight configurable display pages.
- Set the alarm once, every day, selected days, or on a specified interval.

NOTE What BigClock sacrifices in features (and complexity, I might add), it makes up for in being simple to operate. Want more features? Try FPS Clock 2.

Getting Started with Big Clock

To use Time, Alarm, Word, or Timer, just tap the on-screen button. Big-Clock uses the settings on your Visor to coordinate time and date. The table shows the main commands for BigClock.

Menu	Option	Shortcut	What It Does
Options	Set Time	/S	Allows you to set the time
	Layout	/L	Allows complete customization of opening time screens

Menu	Option	Shortcut	What It Does
Options	Alarm	/A	Allows for the setting of four alarms and options such as snooze, backlighting, and auto close (after the alarm goes off)
	World	/W	Allows you to set the time in four different locations (perfect for those time-zone jet-setters)
	Timer	/T	Times how long it takes you to walk to the store or complete that last entry in your consultant's log book
	Reset Data	/R	Resets the data to the original layout
Sounds	Sound 1	/1	Sets sound 1
	Sound 2	/2	Sets sound 2
	Sound 3	/3	Sets sound 3
	Sound 4	/4	Sets sound 4
Info	Help	/H	Gives you help when you need it
	About	/I	Teaches you all about BigClock

36 Turn Your Visor into a Talking Alarm Clock: BugMe!

BugMe! Version 2.81

www.hausofmaus.com

Shareware: $14.95

Alarms are useful, but how about an alarm that not only gets your attention but reminds you why you set the alarm in the first place? Like "Go to class!" or "Feed the dog!" or "Phone home!" That's what BugMe! does. It's a yellow-sticky reminder without the paper and with easy-to-use alarms. You can quickly create a note, then set an alarm for when the note should pop up and bug you. Use Graffiti or the keyboard and have the note pop up in one minute or seven days from now! Amazing.

Getting Started with BugMe!

To enter a note with BugMe! and set the alarm, follow these steps:

1. Either use the pen to scribble your reminder or use Graffiti to enter the note. As you create the text, it appears on the Visor screen. You can choose the pen thickness or select an eraser to rub out mistakes using icons at the bottom of the screen.

2. Set the bug time by choosing either one of the defined durations from the pop-up list or by tapping the trigger box at the top of the screen. This brings up the familiar Time dialog, which lets you select a time and day.

3. To make a new note, tap the icon with the little star on the far left. To delete a page, tap the trashcan and confirm the deletion. (In the shareware version, you cannot create new notes.)

Refer to the table below for at-a-glance command help.

Menu	Command	Shortcut	What It Does
Note	New Note	/N	Starts a new note
	Copy Note	/C	Copies a note
	Delete Note	/D	Deletes a note
	Clear Note	/X	Clears a note
	Beam Note	/B	Beam me up, Scotty! (Beams a note to another Visor)
Options	Preferences	/R	Selects button sizes and alarm preferences
	Font	/O	Selects font size
	Register BugMe!	None	Registers BugMe!
Help	About BugMe!	/A	Tells you about BugMe!

Menu	Command	Shortcut	What It Does
Help	Using BugMe!	/H	Provides help on using BugMe!
Options	Explain Icons	None	Explains icons
	How to Register!	None	Tells you all about BugMe!

37 Put Your Visor in Charge: DateMate

DateMate, Version 1.6.1

www.palmate.com

Shareware: $19.95

Pick one of the following scenarios:

- ◆ forgot your wife's/husband's/honey's birthday.
- ◆ forgot to congratulate the boss on his 10th anniversary with the company.
- ◆ forgot to pay the IRS.

No matter how you look at them, any of these options are not exactly ideal. In fact, they can be downright nasty. You can avoid situations like these with DateMate. While DateMate won't help you come up with ideas for birthday presents (although you can attach notes); it can remind you of the boss's anniversary or of April 15th (aka pay-or-die day). All you do is enter the date of the event, and DateMate will automatically give you a few days' warning before the event so, in the words of DateMate's developers, "you'll have enough time to either buy a decent present or prepare a good excuse for not doing so." The program allows you to just tap the column heading (Name, Date, and Yrs. to sort in descending or ascending order) and tap an event to edit it.

Getting Started with DateMate

You can enter events in DateMate two ways. Here's the first:

1. Tap the New button or select New Event from the Record menu.

2. Enter the following information:

- ◆ Last name

- ◆ First name

- ◆ Date of the event

- ◆ Category in which the event belongs

3. Tap the alarm box if you want an audible reminder.

4. Tap the Note button if you want to attach a note to the reminder.

5. Tap OK, and the event is entered.

The second (and less fun) way is to save the event in the Custom field of the Visor Address Book and then import it into DateMate.

Take a look at the table below for the following DateMate commands.

NOTE Want to add your own categories to DateMate? Just tap the drop-down arrow in the upper-right corner of the screen, tap Edit Categories, and edit or add what you want.

Menu	Command	Shortcut	What It Does
Records	New Event	/N	Creates a new event
	Delete Events	/D	Deletes an event
Edit	Undo	/U	Undoes the last entry
	Cut	/X	Cuts an entry and places it on the Clipboard
	Copy	/C	Copies an entry to the Clipboard
	Paste	/P	Pastes an entry
	Select All	/A	Selects all the information in an event
	Keyboard	/K	Allows you to use the keyboard to enter information
	Graffiti	/G	Allows you to use Graffiti to enter information
Options	About DateMate	None	Tells you all about DateMate

Menu	Command	Shortcut	What It Does
Options	Preferences	/R	Allows you to set preferences for the display of information and categories
	Help	/H	Gives you help when you need it
	Import	/L	Allows you to import information from another application to DateMate
	How to Purchase	None	Instructs you on purchasing DateMate
	Registration	None	Tells you how to register DateMate

38 Turn Your Visor into a Programmable Clock: FPS Clock 2

FPS Clock 2, Version 2, Release 5

www.fps.com

Shareware: $9.95

This is it! Everything you've always wanted in a clock but were afraid to ask for—it's here. FPS offers a large, readable digital clock; a never-sleep feature (so you can use it like a real clock); a snooze alarm that allows you up to 25 minutes of extra z-z-z-z's; a repeatable alarm only on days you choose; and the "infinite" alarm, which can ring up to 254 times. The opening screen lets you define preferences such as military time, number of alarm rings, and more. The most fun part is that you can use the backlight feature as part of the clock's alarm—you can have the backlight flash, leave it on, or use it as a silent alarm.

TIP Just remember that the backlight uses battery power.

Getting Started with FPS Clock 2

Follow these simple steps to use FPS Clock 2:

1. Set the preferences on the opening screen.

2. Go to it using all the options available on the clock screen.

The important commands for FPS Clock 2 appear in this table.

Menu	Option	Shortcut	What It Does
Options	About FPS Clock 2	/A	Tells you all about FPS Clock 2
	Preferences	/P	Allows for the setting of different options such as military time, use of backlight options, and more

39 Use Your Visor as an Analog (Yes, I Said Analog) Clock: RClock

RClock, Version 1

linkesoft.com

Shareware: $10

RClock is a nicely executed and welcome change from the digital madness that seems to have invaded everything. RClock is just like that simple analog clock (displaying your Visor system's time) that used to sit on your grandparents' mantle and even appear on your wrist! Remember those? In addition to a cool little dot that appears around the clock as a second indicator, you can use it as an alarm clock.

Getting Started with RClock

To set the alarm, follow these steps:

1. Tap Menu ➤ Options ➤ Alarm Settings.

2. Drag the clock's "hands" to the time you want the alarm to sound.

3. Tap AM or PM.

Once the alarm is set, you'll see the time it is set for in a little clock in the upper-right corner of RClock. The table that follows shows the main commands for RClock.

Menu	Command	Shortcut	What It Does
Options	Alarm Settings	/A	Sets the alarm
	Show/Hide Seconds	/S	Hides or show seconds
Info	About	None	All about RClock

40 Keep Tabs on How You Are Spending Your Time: TrackFast

TrackFast, Version 1.4b2

www.vision7.com

Commercial software: $30

Does the boss want to know what you did and when you did it? TrackFast is an activity and contact-tracking tool that helps you to organize and keep track of important business relationships, progress toward goals, track completion of assigned tasks, and prepare for events. TrackFast adds value to the already-available Visor tools, since it tracks activities so you can track your progress. One of the most unique and useful things about TrackFast is that you can establish links to existing entries in the Address Book, Date Book, To Do List, and Memo Pad. And what could be better than a keyword and name completion feature so that with just a few strokes of the stylus, frequently used phrases are entered.

TrackFast organizes activities into Tracks and Entries with Tracks being the highest level of organization. A Track can be created for anything (birthday, business meeting, appointments) or whatever needs monitoring over a period of time. In turn, each Track contains a list of Entries.

Getting Started with TrackFast

Using TrackFast consists of first creating a track and then creating an entry. It's the entries that keep the information about your particular activities. To create a track, follow these steps:

1. Tap the New button to bring up the New Track dialog. Enter a title for your sample track.

2. Tap the Save button to save the track and return to the Tracks view.

To create an Entry, follow these steps:

1. In the Tracks view, tap the empty arrow symbol to the left of the Track title or tap the Open button.

2. Tap the New button to create an empty Entry with today's date.

3. Tap the Time triangle (▼).

4. Select Choose Time from the drop-down menu.

5. Define the time allocated for the activity by clicking on the hour and minute, and click OK.

6. Enter a description of the activity.

7. Tap Done.

This table shows a list of commands for TrackFast.

Menu	Option	Shortcut	What It Does
Options	Keywords	/Y	Adds and removes frequently used words
	Help	/H	Help on TrackFast
	About TrackFast	/A	All about TrackFast
Entries	Save to Memo	/S	Saves a memo
	Purge	/P	Purges an entry

41 Can't Figure Out Why Your Phone Bill Is so High: PhoneLog

PhoneLog, Version 2.04

www.handshigh.com

Commercial software: $19.95

It's hard enough to manage remembering the milk on the way home or the paper due tomorrow (try BugMe! on the companion CD-ROM), but remembering who telephoned and how much time you spent with them is enough to drive anyone batty. PhoneLog helps to manage your phone activities and does things such as:

- ◆ Prioritize your follow-up.

- ◆ Sort and manage your calls by contact, project, or action you want to take.

- ◆ Create custom type and subject lists.

- ◆ Easily categorize your calls.

- ◆ Time your calls by simply tapping the Start button.

- ◆ Keep track of how much your neighbor who just asked you for legal advice should be charged!

You can also use it to track billing, perfect for when the client calls and the clock starts.

Getting Started with PhoneLog

To enter a phone contact, follow these steps:

1. Click the New button.

2. Enter the name of the contact, phone number, and any additional information you feel is important.

3. Click the Start button to track time spent with the client.

4. Tap the Return icon to enter the client information in the PhoneLog list.

The commands for PhoneLog are listed in this table.

Menu	Commands	What It Does
Options	Preferences	Allows you to define QuickFill options, order of last and first names, and whether initial list shows name or phone number
	Export to Memo Pad	Exports the list of phone information to a Memo Pad document
	Purge	Purges an entry
	About PhoneLog	All about PhoneLog

42 So, When Is the Big Game: AnySchedule

AnySchedule

www.quantumlynx.com/anyschedule

Shareware: $15

OK. Admit it. You're a sports junky. And what Visor aficionado who is a sports junky doesn't have the season schedules for every conceivable sporting event right at his or her fingertips? AnySchedule can do more to ruin your marriage or relationship than any other Visor application. Just make sure you have enough popcorn and other treats to go around.

AnySchedule works with schedules (each one being a .pdb file) that are downloaded to your Visor. What schedules you might ask? Try these on for size:

- ◆ Major League Baseball
- ◆ PGA Golf
- ◆ LPGA Golf
- ◆ Senior PGA Golf
- ◆ European PGA
- ◆ NFL Football
- ◆ College Football
- ◆ WNBA Basketball
- ◆ Indy Racing (Indy Racing 2000 Schedule)
- ◆ Rugby World Cup
- ◆ NBA Basketball
- ◆ American Hockey League
- ◆ Big Ten College Basketball

And that's just a sample from the many more which are available.

Other features? You can create your own schedules and beam schedules to other Visor users. Just think— You'll never be late for the Yankees-Mets subway series!

```
AnySchedule
New York Knicks 1999-2000

 2000/Feb/01    7:30pmE

Event: Orlando at New York


Location: New York


Other: |

Events Selected:
ALL EVENTS                          ⬆
New  Del  GoTo  Browse  Close      ⬇
```

Getting Started with AnySchedule

To use AnySchedule, you need to load the basic application as well as whatever schedules you want to use. When the basic application is open, the schedules will appear as well. Tap on the schedule you want to use. See this chart for AnySchedule's commands.

Menu	Command	Shortcut	What It Does
Options	Select All Records	/a	Selects all records
	Events Containing	/e	Searches for records containing
	Location Containing	/i	Searches by location for records
	Other Containing	/o	Searches by other field for records
	Copyright Notice	/c	Undoes most recent operation

43 Does Anyone Know What Time It Is: CityTime

CityTime, Version 2.53a

www.codecity.com.au

Freeware

If you've ever wondered what time it really is (and what time the sunrise and sunset will be anywhere on the planet), CityTime has that information and more. And what's especially cool is that it comes as part of the

ROM (built-in memory) on all Visors that were manufactured after September 14, 1999. So if you got your Visor since then, you already have City-Time. CityTime is the major league global/world/galaxy/universe timekeeper that includes:

◆ Day and night times shown across the world in real time (so you know it will be dark when you get there).

◆ Just tap on the screen anywhere in the world and you can estimate the time and location to the nearest city. Four world clocks on-screen give precise information and show day of week as well.

◆ Number of hours of daylight wherever on earth on whatever day you want.

◆ Add and delete cities.

◆ See the Visor's date and time when traveling to other time zones.

◆ Fully automatic daylight savings time.

Getting Started with CityTime

To set a new home city, follow these steps:

1. Tap the Menu Visor button.

2. Tap Utilities ➢ Change Location.

3. Select a new city from the down arrow for which you want the time.

4. Tap OK.

See the table below for some command shortcuts.

N O T E   You can define four world clocks on the opening screen by just tapping one of the down arrows and selecting another city. So if your itinerary is Paris, Dubai, Moscow, and finally Manilla, you'll know exactly what time the sun rises and sets. Happy traveling.

Menu	Command	Shortcut	What It Does
Options	Help	None	Provides CityTime Help
	Select Home City	/H	Selects the home city
	Edit Cities	/E	Edits and lets you add new cities
	Register	None	Registers CityTime
	About City Time	/A	About CityTime
Utilities	Preferences	/R	Sets preferences
	Change Location	/L	Changes current location
	Time Calculator	/T	Calculates time in different locations
	Sun Rise/Sun Set	/S	Allows you to examine times in different locations
	Keyboard	/K	Uses the keyboard to enter information
	Graffiti	/G	Uses Graffiti to enter information

Communications Anywhere, Anytime

What you'll read about (and hopefully explore here) is maybe the most remarkable set of applications you could imagine for the Visor. Imagine sitting at your desk at work before your commute home and thinking about what material you'll catch up with during the long commute home. You search your favorite Boston Red Sox sites on the Web, download the content of the pages and, with a Visor-based Web browser, read to your heart's content.

It's not "real" time since you're not actually connected to the Web, but it's the next best thing—the Web at your fingertips through your Visor.

44 Store the Web on Your Visor: AvantGo

AvantGo Client, Version 3

www.avantgo.com

Freeware

Clever is an understatement when it comes to describing what AvantGo can do for you and your Visor. Imagine this. You spend time at your PC or Mac, looking at Web sites and finding the best information about investing, sports, gardening, etc. And then you have that long commute on the train and you wish that you could take those Web sites with you. Well, with AvantGo, you can take information from the Web and put it directly onto your Visor. Simply choose the Web sites (or channels, as the AvantGo people call them) that you would like to transfer to your Visor from the AvantGo Web site, and then HotSync. You now have another way and another reason why the Visor is slowly replacing almost everything the traditional laptop can do. Wonder of wonders.

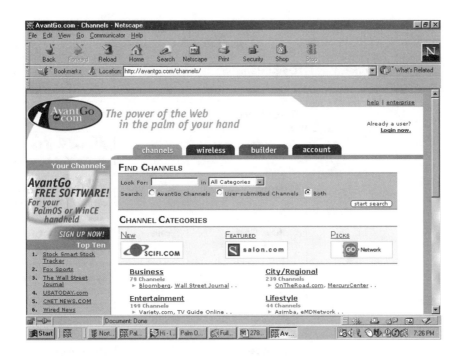

AvantGo has become very popular with hundreds of channels on the Web site, and the user reviews have been outstanding. This is certainly a must-have application.

Getting Started with AvantGo Client

To use AvantGo, follow these steps:

1. Download and install AvantGo on your desktop computer. It installs much like any Windows- or Mac-based program.

2. From the Web site at www.avantgo.com, select the channels you want to view, such as the one for www.visorcentral.com, a Web site with Visor-specific information.

3. Select the information that you want to transfer from the Web site to your Visor.

4. HotSync to make the transfer.

The following table shows a chart with the latest commands for AvantGo.

Menu	Command	Shortcut	What It Does
Channels	Open Page	/O	Opens a page for a particular URL
	Reload Page	/L	Reloads the current page
	Forms Manager	/M	Allows you to manage already loaded forms
	Channel Manager	None	Allows you to manage already loaded channels
	Online Cache Manager	None	Allows you to manage the online cache
	Modem Sync	None	Synchronizes with your modem
	Connect	None	Connects to the desktop
	Disconnect	None	Disconnects from the desktop
Edit	Cut	/X	Cuts information
	Copy	/C	Copies information
	Paste	/P	Pastes information
	Select All	/S	Selects all the information in a site
	Find	/F	Finds information
	Find Again	/A	Finds the same information again
	Increase Font	None	Makes the on-screen font appear bigger
	Decrease Font	None	Makes the on-screen font appear smaller

Menu	Command	Shortcut	What It Does
Edit	Keyboard	/K	Uses the keyboard for entering information
	Graffiti Help	/G	Gets graffiti help for entering information
Go	Home	/H	Goes to the AvantGo home page
	Back	/B	Goes back one page on your Visor
	Forward	/W	Goes forward one page on your Visor
Options	Preferences	/R	Selects preferences such as showing images and tables
	Server Preferences	None	Selects server preferences
	Font Preferences	None	Selects default font preferences
	About AvantGo	None	All about AvantGo

45 Phone Home (again) from Anywhere: PocketCall

PocketCall, Version 1

www.electricpocket.com

Shareware: $14.95

Yes, it had to happen. Not only can you make a long distance call on your cell phone, but you can use your Visor as well, with one of the cell phone plug-ins, and you can now use your Visor as a pre-paid calling card to make long distance calls! What? You read it here. Electric Pocket's PocketCall makes it far easier to use a calling card phone service and can save you up to 70 percent on calls. There are four sources of information you need to make a call, and they can all be kept in your Visor. They are

◆ The country access code

◆ P.I.N. number

◆ International country code

◆ The numbers (both your number and the number you are dialing)

```
┌─────────────────────────────────────┐
│ PocketCall Pre-Paid                  │
├─────────────────────────────────────┤
│ Calling from:  ▼ US                  │
│ Call is to:    ▼ UK                  │
│ Number: [🔍]|.......................  │
│                                      │
│ To make the call:                    │
│  Dial:  1-888-879-6680               │
│  Enter: 72727272727 Press: #         │
│  Enter: PIN           Press: #4      │
│  Enter: 44 + Number    [?]           │
│  Press: #              ( Help )      │
└─────────────────────────────────────┘
```

Getting Started with PocketCall

PocketCall is cool, but it takes some time to get up and running. Follow these steps to start off:

1. Activate PocketCall by calling the telephone help line. The PocketCall Pre-Paid application gives the telephone number (which will depend on where you are calling from).

2. Enter information about your phone call. The lower section is a "dialing script" that tells you what you need to dial to make a call using the PocketCall Pre-Paid service.

3. To begin making a call, select the country that you are calling from and the country that you are calling. Finally, enter the telephone number of the person you are calling or find it in your Palm Address Book by pressing the "magnifying glass" on the main screen.

4. For further information, follow the instructions in the lower half of the PocketCall Pre-Paid screen—under the heading "To make the call."

Here are some commands for PocketCall.

Menu	Command	Shortcut	What It Does
Service	Activate Your Account	None	Activates your PocketCall account
	Account Balance	None	Shows your PocketCall balance
	Account Recharging	None	Recharges your PocketCall balance
	Phonebook lookup	None	Looks up phone numbers in the Visor Phonebook
	Change Card Number	None	Changes the card number for charging
	Customer Service	None	Accesses customer service
Edit	Undo	/U	Undoes most recent operation
	Cut	/X	Removes information
	Copy	/C	Copies information
	Paste	/V	Pastes information

Menu	Command	Shortcut	What It Does
Edit	Select All	/S	Selects all information
	Keyboard	/K	Uses the keyboard to enter information
	Graffiti Help	/G	Gets Graffiti Help
Help	What is PocketCall?	None	Tells you about PocketCall
	How to activate the service	None	Explains how to activate the PocketCall service
	How to make a call	None	Explains how to make a call using PocketCall
	Customer Service	None	Tells you how to contact customer service (for free) ☺
	Other Telephony Services	None	Summarizes other telephone services that are available
	About Electric Pocket	None	All about Electric Pocket
	About Virtel	None	All about Virtel—the company that provides the home connection for PocketCall
	About PocketCall	None	All about PocketCall

Say What You Mean and Mean What you Say

Remember the paperless office? Fifteen years ago, it was all the talk. The idea was that once personal computers really took hold in the home and workplace, then hard copies of everything would be obsolete—documents would just blast from one office to another or from home to school. OK, so it didn't happen. There's more paper than ever. Just go ask a tree in the old-growth forest.

However, technology today can bring us new ways to look at words, be they books, magazines, or office documents. One way is through the use of a document reader such as AportisDoc. Whether on your treadmill, the train home, or at the campsite late at night (with your very cool Visor backlit screen), you can download and read e-books galore—from *Treasure Island* to *Tom Swift*.

46 Read E-Books on Your Visor: AportisDoc

AportisDoc, Version 2.1

www.aportis.com

Shareware: $30

AportisDoc illustrates just one of the reasons why the Visor is such a great tool for gaining access to information. AportisDoc, which is the industry standard, allows you to read any document on your Visor—even a book! Imagine having the data for a particular project or the service manual for a particular client's mechanical configuration at your fingertips. Don't try to read your Visor while you're driving, but on the commute or at 30,000 feet, all of H. G. Wells' *Time Machine* can be right there for you on your Visor. The possibilities for this Visor application make for endless fun.

AportisDoc used to come in three versions, but now only the Professional version is available (as if you needed more!). It's the top of the line reader, easy to use, and incredibly powerful. It's even a cinch to place your own writing on your Visor.

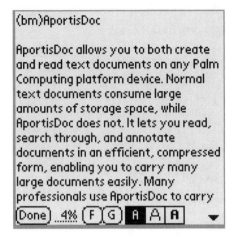

Getting Started with AportisDoc

To read a document using this reader, you have to install the reader files (ApotisDoc.prc and AdocReference.pdb) and then install whatever document you want to read on your Visor. Here are some of the basics:

1. Double-tap in the List screen on the doc you want to read.

2. Tap the screen to scroll to the next page or press the Up or Down button on your Visor. You can even set the Prompter to automatically scroll for you.

3. Tap the Done button when you are done reading a document. Even though you may go to another document, AportisDoc will save your place.

There are an increasing number of locations on the Internet where you can find documents in doc format. The best is MemoWare (thanks to Craig Froehle) at www.memoware.com, which contains hundreds (and hundreds and hundreds) of documents in categories (and subcategories) including (Yikes! Look at all these!):

Business

◆ Career

◆ Communications

- ◆ Computers
- ◆ Engineering
- ◆ Entertainment
- ◆ Food & Nutrition
- ◆ History
- ◆ Law & Gov't
- ◆ Math & Science
- ◆ Medicine
- ◆ Miscellaneous
- ◆ Palm-Related
- ◆ Philosophy
- ◆ Religion
- ◆ Sports
- ◆ Travel

Literature

- ◆ Adventure
- ◆ Biography
- ◆ Children's
- ◆ Horror
- ◆ Humor
- ◆ Literature
- ◆ Mystery
- ◆ Novels
- ◆ Poetry
- ◆ Romance
- ◆ Sci-Fi
- ◆ Shakespeare

- ◆ Short Story
- ◆ Theater
- ◆ Western
- ◆ eZines
- ◆ AuthorSearch
- ◆ Contemporary Books

Links

- ◆ Accessories
- ◆ Development
- ◆ Fiction
- ◆ Homepages
- ◆ Other
- ◆ Price Compare
- ◆ Services
- ◆ Software

Help

- ◆ Main Help
- ◆ File Formats
- ◆ Adding to Palm
- ◆ Making DOCs
- ◆ Contributing
- ◆ Psion Owners
- ◆ Avigo Owners
- ◆ Newton Owners
- ◆ WinCE Owners

Want more? Mary Jo's E-texts files has stuff for kids, including most of the Oz books and the Brothers Grimm, at `dogpatch.org/etext.html`. In the meantime, you can check out AportisDoc's main commands in the table below.

Menu	Option	Shortcut	What It Does
Options	About AportisDoc	/Q	All about AportisDoc
	Preferences	/Z	Allows you to set preferences for how you want text to appear
	Copy	/C	Copies text
	Close Document	/W	Closes the current document
	Details	/I	Details about the document itself
Go	Find	/F	Finds text
	Find Again	/O	Finds the same text again
	GoTo BookMark	/M	Goes to a defined bookmark
	Add Bookmark	/R	Creates a bookmark
	Delete Bookmark	//	Deletes a bookmark
	AutoBookmark	/Y	Enters text in a dialog box and bookmarks it throughout the document
	To Top	/<	Goes to top of the document
	To Bottom	/>	Goes to bottom of the document
Display	Start Prompter	/T	Starts the prompter
	Stop Prompter	/H	Stops the prompter

Menu	Option	Shortcut	What It Does
Display	Set Up Prompter	/N	Selects the time you want to use for the prompter to go to a new page or line
	Larger text Window	/+	Increases text size
	Smaller text Window	/-	Decreases text size
	Regular Font	/1	Uses a regular font
	Big Font	/2	Uses a large font
	Bold Font	/3	Uses a bolded font
	Monospaced	/4	Uses a proportional font
	Screen Width	/E	Sets the screen width

47 Read Spreadsheets on Your Visor: Documents To Go

Documents To Go, Version 2.505

www.dataviz.com

Commercial software: $39.95

There are many applications, such as AportisDoc, that allow you to read documents on your Visor. Documents To Go is another such application, this time from DataViz. Where it stands out from the others is that it can transfer (without any conversion on your part) both word processing and spreadsheet documents easily and accurately and read them on your Visor.

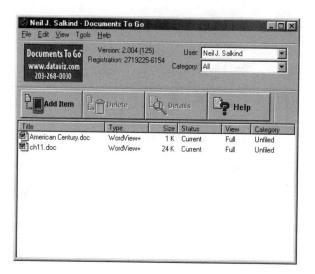

Getting Started with Documents To Go

To move a document from your desktop to the Visor, follow these steps:

1. Open the Documents To Go program on your desktop.

2. Drag the file representing the document into the Documents To Go window or click the Add Item button to select the file

3. HotSync, and the document will be on the Visor.

Additionally, here are some tips for working with word processing documents on your Visor:

◆ Tap on the top half of the document to scroll up, and on the bottom half to scroll down.

◆ To scroll continuously, tap and hold on the bottom half of the document.

◆ To go to a different part of the document, tap on the drop-down percentage menu and identify where you want to go to.

◆ Use the Find and Find Again features by first tapping the menu and then selecting the option you want to use.

And try these tips for working with spreadsheet documents on your Visor:

◆ To move to the next range of cells in a spreadsheet, drag the stylus up, down, left, right, or diagonally.

◆ To get to a particular cell, tap the Go command.

◆ To move between different spreadsheets, tap the drop-down menu on the top-right portion on the screen.

◆ To freeze cells or adjust column width, tap on a column header.

Check out the following table for Documents To Go's key commands.

Menu	Command	Shortcut	What It Does
Record	Delete Item	/D	Deletes an item
Options	Find Viewer Add-ons	/A	Selects the type of document to be viewed
	About Documents To Go	None	All about Documents To Go

48 A Language That's Easier than Graffiti: Thumbscript

Thumbscript, Version 1.1

www.thumbscript.com

Freeware

It had to happen. First there was the stylus for writing on your Visor, then came the keyboard (see the GoType!Pro description on page 17), and now you can enter characters using a single stroke for anything you can find on a computer keyboard. Thumbscript is a visual keypad alphabet, based on the nine keys on your phone, or in the case of the Visor, an array of nine dots on your screen. It is a little like Graffiti, but still quite a bit different and very unique.

Thumbscript works like this. Think of the keypad you use as a simple drawing tablet consisting of nine dots representing a numeric keypad with one in the upper-left corner and nine in the lower-right corner of your keypad. You use that drawing tablet to construct letters. For example, to enter an *a*, press the 7 key, then the 9 key. Drawing other letters is similar. You press the start key (indicated by a dot) and then the stop key at the end of the letter. In this way, each character is defined by a two-stroke key sequence. All letters are drawn from one of the outer buttons to the center and back to an outer button; all letters are drawn from top to bottom, or if start and stop are on the same line, then from left to right; and the vowels e, i, o, u are drawn with a straight line through the center. Any character including letters and numerals can be drawn with the same two strokes.

Characters

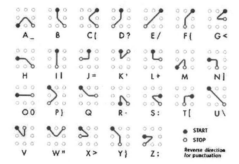

What is special for the Visor is that the software doesn't care what you do between start and stop, so once you know the alphabet, you can draw one straight stroke from start to stop. The developers claim that once mastered, one can draw 25 percent faster than using Graffiti, and the demo contained on the disk lets you practice making brief notes or messages. And if you really want to be the first one on your block, join Friends of Thumbscript at http://www.thumbscript.com/friends.html.

49 Improve Your Speed in Graffiti: WPM

WPM, Version 0.96

www.ddhsoftware.com

Freeware

Ever wonder how those other people in your office use *only* their Visor for everything, including taking notes at a furious speed? One way is that they practice using Giraffe, the built-in application used to increase speed and accuracy that comes with the Visor. Another way is by using WPM, which allows you to measure just how fast your word entry and accuracy skills are.

This is a very simple program that requires you to copy text provided by the program. You get a words-per-minute reading, as well as several other features that make WPM even more useful, such as

◆ You can enter your own sentences and time your entry. This is a good option if you have fixed phrases that you frequently use.

◆ Just like PacMan and Asteroid, there's a list of high scorers (WPM Scorers), allowing you to chart your improvement.

Getting Started with WPM

Here are the basics:

1. Tap the Start button.

2. Using Graffiti, enter the text that is shown on the top of the screen.

3. Tap the Done button and read your words-per-minute score.

The following table shows the commands that will get you typing in no time.

Menu	Command	Shortcut	What It Does
File	Set Sentence	/S	Creates a sentence to practice with
	View Stats	/V	To see the highest-scoring users
Edit	Cut	/X	Cuts text from a sentence
	Copy	/C	Copies text from a sentence
	Paste	/P	Pastes text into a sentence
	Keyboard	/K	Uses the keyboard to create text to use with WPM
About	About	/A	All about WPM

50 Check Your Spelling: SpellMan

SpellMan, Version 1.01

www.standalone.com

Commercial software: $15

SpellMan does just what it says—it checks the spelling of a Visor document and provides you with alternatives as to what word you can use.

Getting Started with SpellMan

To check the spelling in any document (Memo Pad, To Do list, etc.), follow these steps:

1. Place a question mark (?) at the beginning of the text to check the entire document.

2. As SpellMan finds words that it does not recognize, you can either add them to the dictionary, correct them, or select from a list of suggestions as a replacement.

NOTE In order to use SpellMan, you must download the SpellMan file, plus either the long or short word database including both a–m and n–z. The long word list contains over 100,000 words and takes about 500k on your Visor. The short option takes up only 330k and it contains only those words from the set that are 4–9 characters in length.

In addition to the spelling check, SpellMan is very flexible and, by first tapping on the SpellMan icon, you can make all kinds of adjustments, such as:

◆ You can have the program warn you when it does not recognize a word and give suggestions of alternate spellings.

- ◆ You can have the program automatically capitalize unknown words.
- ◆ You can have it look up a word ending in a "?" to check specific words.
- ◆ You can have SpellMan not check words with capital letters or punctuation.
- ◆ You can also delete words that you added to the dictionary. Tap the Edit User Word List button and tap the word you wish to delete.

WARNING   Using a spell checker does not stop you from misusing words, right? It's too easy to assume otherwise, right?

The table below shows some specific commands and shortcuts to use with SpellMan.

Menu	Command	What It Does
Options	Enter Password	Enters the password sent when registered
	About SpellMan	All about SpellMan

51 A Tool to Bring Life to Your Words: Thesaurus

Thesaurus, Version 1.11

www.ddhsoftware.com/ddhthes.html

Shareware: $15

Let's see—the word I'm looking for is kind of, sorta, almost like, treasure, but not quite. How about windfall, prize, blessing, boon, assets, cash, or 26 others just for this word? That's what a thesaurus, and this Thesaurus, does for you: It finds words with the same meaning. This is an extraordinarily useful tool for people who regularly write on their Visor—which more and more users are doing. In fact with tools like GoType!, people are using the Visor as their main text entry tool.

Here are just some of the features:

◆ 50,000 entries cross-referenced and indexed for speed

◆ Forward and Back, Rewind, and Fast Forward buttons for browsing through the alphabetical list of entries and their synonyms

◆ The last 15 words that were looked up memorized and shown in a quick pop-up history list

◆ Display of all synonyms, or just nouns, verbs, adjectives, or adverbs

◆ User-adjustable number of maximum matches, ranging from 5 (for speed) to 80 matches (for depth)

◆ Two modes: Thesaurus/Dictionary and SpellCheck

Getting Started with Thesaurus

To use the Thesaurus/Dictionary mode:

1. Write a word on the line and tap Find Word. A list of synonyms will appear in the box below.

2. To look up a word from within MemoPad, highlight the word and choose Copy.

3. Run the Thesaurus program, and Thesaurus will automatically find synonyms for the word in the Copy/Paste buffer.

Select a synonym by tapping it in the list box. It will automatically be in SpellCheck mode:

4. Write a word on the line and hit Find Word. If the word is spelled correctly, you will see the message Correct Spelling! If it is not in the dictionary, the program will suggest similarly spelled words.

To check the spelling of a word in MemoPad, follow these steps:

1. Highlight the word.

2. Tap Menu, then tap Copy.

3. Start the Thesaurus program. If Thesaurus finds an exact match, it will show Correct Spelling! If not, it will suggest several words of proper spelling. Select the appropriate word by touching it in the list box. Go back to the MemoPad application and select Paste.

Interested in being a better writer? Thesaurus is a tool (or utensil or apparatus or appliance) you should not miss. This table shows some commands for Thesaurus.

Menu	Command	Shortcut	What It Does
Options	Preferences	/R	Customizes Thesaurus
Edit	Cut	/X	Cuts information to Thesaurus

Menu	Command	Shortcut	What It Does
Edit	Copy	/C	Copies information to Thesaurus
	Paste	/P	Pastes information into Thesaurus
	Keyboard	/K	Uses the keyboard to create information
About	About	/R	About Thesaurus

52 Get the Scoop on Computer Jargon: MIT New Hacker's Dictionary

MIT New Hacker's Dictionary, Version 4

http://www.handango.com/product.shtml?sectionId=376&productId=1392

Shareware: $15

This is an add-on to whatever application you use to read documents (I use AportisDoc), including commentaries, myths, and definitions about the jargon that now surrounds the computer world. This is not your mother's or father's dictionary—for the most part it is a stream of thoughts about where computers have come from, where they are, and where they are going. Informative and well organized, the New Hacker's Dictionary is the most fun to browse of any of the e-Book materials available.

Getting Started with MIT New Hacker's Dictionary

To use the hacker's dictionary, follow these steps:

1. Open AportisDoc or whatever document reader you want to use.

2. Tap the MIT New Hacker's Dictionary icon.

3. Read away!

The table below focuses on MIT New Hacker's Dictionary key commands.

Menu	Option	Shortcut	What It Does
Options	About AportisDoc	/Q	All about AportisDoc
	Preferences	/Z	Allows you to set preferences for how you want text to appear
	Copy	/C	Copies text
	Close Document	/W	Closes the current document
	Details	/I	Details about the document itself
Go	Find	/F	Finds text
	Find Again	/O	Finds the same text again
	GoTo BookMark	/M	Goes to a defined bookmark
	Add Bookmark	/R	Creates a bookmark
	Delete Bookmark	//	Deletes a bookmark
	AutoBookmark	/Y	Enters text in a dialog box and bookmarks it throughout the document

Menu	Option	Shortcut	What It Does
Go	To Top	/<	Goes to top of the document
	To Bottom	/>	Goes to bottom of the document
Display	Start Prompter	/T	Starts the prompter
	Stop Prompter	/H	Stops the prompter
	Set Up Prompter	/N	Selects the time you want to use for the prompter to go to a new page or line
	Larger text Window	/+	Increases text size
	Smaller text Window	/-	Decreases text size
	Regular Font	/1	Uses a regular font
	Big Font	/2	Uses a large font
	Bold Font	/3	Uses a bolded font
	Monospaced	/4	Uses a proportional font
	Screen Width	/E	Sets the screen width

53 Hola! or Hello: Translate

Translate

www.ddhsoftware.com

Commercial software: $70

Who needs to take foreign language classes? With Translate, you can enter a word in any one of many different languages (such as Danish, French, Spanish, Mandarin, Latin, Japanese, and of course Indonesian) and get a translation of what you enter on the screen in seconds.

Will this be able to help you act as an interpreter and settle conflicts in the Balkans? No. Will it help you ask, "Where is the bathroom"? Definitely. This is a very handy and comprehensive tool for performing translations and can even translate sentences. To find out how to say "Where is the bathroom?" see the graphic below.

Among the features you will find

◆ Translations between English and 18 different languages.

◆ Each language is available separately.

◆ There are buttons to go forward or backward one in either language, as well as buttons to go to the first and last word in either language.

◆ You can edit and add entries.

◆ Allows Translation of both phrases and sentences.

Getting Started with Translate

This is easy. Just enter the word or phrase you want to translate and click the button naming the language into which you want the words translated. Translate has only a couple of commands, as shown in the following table.

Menu	Command	Shortcut	What It Does
File	Choose Language	/H	Selects a language
	Preferences	/R	Defines preferences
Edit	Cut	/X	Removes information
	Copy	/C	Copies information
	Paste	/P	Pastes information
	Keyboard	/K	Uses the keyboard to enter information
About	About	/A	About Translate

Lifelong Learning and Your Visor: Education

It's true. The more active your mind (and body), the longer you'll probably live and the happier you will be. And with the baby boomer retirement right on the horizon, we should all take all the learning opportunities we can.

Your Visor can more than carry the day in this department. There is an endless set of Visor programs that will enrich your life, help you find new hobbies, and just teach you what you didn't know before. And to think, your Visor runs on only two AAA batteries!

54 Browse the Periodic Table of Elements: Element

Element, Version 1.5.2

www.mindgear.com/element/index.html

Shareware: $18

Remember that huge chart at the front of your chemistry class and all those numbers and symbols? Well, now it's on your Visor and it's a straightforward and easy-to-use presentation of the periodic table. The table appears on a single screen, and information about a selected element is displayed in a scroll display at the bottom of the screen. You can select an element by tapping it directly in the table, or by entering its name, symbol, weight, or atomic number. And this is no lightweight compilation of data—for each element, 25 properties are available. It's also easy to identify groups of elements with related properties.

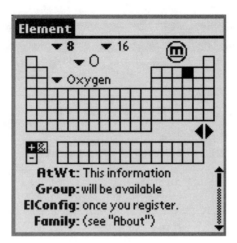

Getting Started with Element

Follow these steps to use Element:

1. Tap a box in the table to select an element and display all of its properties.

2. Above the table display are four fields, which are:

◆ Atomic Number (top-left)

◆ Mass Number (top-right)

◆ Symbol (center)

◆ Element Name (bottom)

Tapping on any of these fields will display a sorted pop-up list from which you can select elements by that property.

3. Right below the periodic table is a list of 21 additional properties of the selected element.

The important commands for Element are shown in the following chart.

Menu	Command	Shortcut	What It Does
Edit	Undo	/U	Undoes the last operation
	Copy	/C	Copies information to the clipboard
Mark	Selected	/M	Used to mark elements
	All	/A	Used to mark all elements
	None	/N	Used to mark no elements
	Equal	/E	Use this Boolean operator to search for new elements
	Greater	/G	Use this Boolean operator to search for new elements
	Less	/L	Use this Boolean operator to search for new elements
Options	Property Information	/I	Information about the properties described in element.
	About Element	None	All about Element

55 Create Your Own Flash Cards: Flash!

Flash! Version 2.0.8

homunculus.dragonfire.net/flash.html

Shareware: $12.95

Flash cards work on one of the most basic assumptions of how people learn: immediate feedback. And Flash! is just the program to do it. It presents a deck of flash cards that you create. Each of the cards is presented to you on your Visor and then you answer the question—in multiple-choice format or whatever format you choose—and then see if you are right or wrong. Flash! tracks your correct and incorrect answers and also offers the following, rather ingenious and useful features:

◆ Import databases from MemoPad or BrainForest (a major time saver)

◆ Share decks with other Visor and Flash! users

◆ Use already created decks on teaching yourself Japanese and Spanish

◆ Merge decks

◆ Create a multiple-choice format

◆ Run tests of multiple decks

Morse code	▼ Unfiled 🗐
E	o
T	-
I	oo
A	o-
N	-o
M	--
S	ooo
U	oo-
D	-oo
W	o--
K	-o-

Qs this deck:0   Rs:0   Ws:0

🏠🖊↘ (New) (Details)   ◆▼

NOTE   Also notable is that half of all the income from Flash! goes to charities generally dealing with low-income education and hunger in the U.S. and abroad.

Getting Started with Flash!

To create a deck, follow these steps:

1. Tap the New button on the list view (the view with the house highlighted in the lower-left corner) to create a deck.

2. Enter the name of the deck and the preferences and tap the OK button.

3. Tap the New button to create a card.

4. Enter the question. To enter the answer to this question, first hit the exclamation point at the upper right and then enter the answer.

5. Tap the New button again to create a new card.

Check out Flash's key commands below.

Menu	Command	Shortcut	What It Does
Deck	New Deck	/K	Starts a new deck
	Delete Deck	/D	Deletes an existing deck
	Deck Details	/T	Shows the details about a deck, including title and latest test score
	End Current test	/E	Ends the current test
	New Test	/N	Starts a new test
Options	About Flash!	None	All about Flash!
	Preferences	/F	Selects font and various display options
	Register	None	Registers Flash!

56 Generate Random Numbers: Handy Randy

Handy Randy, Version 1.1

www.stevenscreek.com/pilot/dodownload.html

Shareware: $14.95

Now you must be asking yourself, "why would I ever need to generate random numbers (numbers that are completely independent from one another) and what does this have to do with education?" Lots of reasons really. How about assigning random numbers to determine who out of a large group of people participates in an experiment? Or selecting the winner of a prize or lottery? Or, using them to assign people to heats in a race. Handy Randy is a cinch for generating random numbers; all you do is tap the Draw a Number button and the random numbers appear. Using the settings option you can also:

- ◆ Generate and display random numbers in user-specifiable ranges (e.g., 1-1000)

- ◆ Specify up to nine different, non-contiguous ranges (e.g., 1-200, 350-475) from which to select your numbers

- ◆ Track all numbers drawn

- ◆ Option to draw or not draw the same number twice

- ◆ Specify how many numbers are drawn with each tap, from 1 to 999

- ◆ Generate random numbers up to eight digits in size

- ◆ Sort numbers into numerical order

- ◆ Display the entire list of numbers which have been drawn

And the icing on this cake is that you can use PalmPrint from the same people (StevensCreek Software) to print out your list of random numbers.

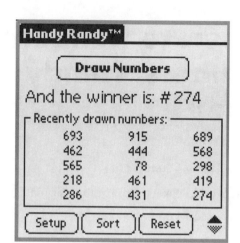

Getting Started with Handy Randy

Tap the Draw a Number button on the opening screen and you'll see a random number! (Devilishly simple and devilishly random!) Or, tap Setup and define the number and range of random numbers that you want to use. The following chart will help you with Handy Randy's commands.

Menu	Command	Shortcut	What It Does
Options	Print	/P	Prints the list of generated numbers
	About Handy Randy	None	All about Handy Randy

57 Loss for Inspiration: Mahatma Gandhi's Quotes

Mahatma Gandhi's Quotes

www.coslink.net/PalmaSrv

Document/Add-In Software

Want some tips on overthrowing a hundreds of years old colonial imperialist government? Turn to Mahatma Gandhi's Quotes for 250 quotes that can surely get you started. These quotes require you to install the iSilo reader located at www.isilo.com. iSilo, just like AportisDoc, allows you to read text on your Visor.

> ▪ Each one has to find his **peace** from within. And peace to be real must be unaffected by outside circumstances.
>
> ▪ It is man's social nature which distinguishes him from the brute creation. If it is his privilege to be independent, it is equally his duty to be inter-dependent. Only an arrogant man will claim to be independent of everybody else and be self-contained.
>
> (Done) (Find)(Next)　　　(51%)

Getting Started with Mahatma Gandhi's Quotes

1. Be sure that you have installed the iSilo reader as well as Mahatma Gandhi's Quotes.

2. Tap Mahatma Gandhi's Quotes.

3. Tap Find to search for a quote containing specific words.

4. Tap next to go to the next quote in the stack.

The chart below shows the key commands for Mahatma Gandhi's Quotes.

Menu	Command	Shortcut	What It Does
Commands	Preferences	/P	Define font and scrollbar action
	Details	/D	Edit quote bank
	About iSilo Free	/R	About iSilo Free
Marks	Mark Location	/M	Mark current quote
	Jump to Mark	/J	Jump to a marked quote

58 Er – Where's My Homework: Due Yesterday

Due Yesterday, Version 2.11

www.nosleep.net

Shareware: $10

This might be the #1 Visor application for students – it tracks just about everything about your school assignments including what is due when, the points that its worth and more. Just look at what you can specify for that nuclear physics class:

◆ Description of the class and point value

◆ Due date and time

- One-tap access to due yesterday's most important features
- Organize assignments by category
- Weight the assignment and find out your position in any given class

The important opening screen buttons allow you to create new assignments, work with class grades (but not change them ☺), look for what's due next, get class information, explore program options, and get details on any one assignment.

What more do you need to be an A student than this?

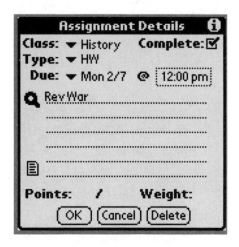

Getting Started with Due Yesterday

Due Yesterday is powerful and has many different options. The program comes with a terrific set of documents in Acrobat PDF format so it looks just like a real live manual. We'll show you how to get started entering an assignment:

1. Tap the drop-down menu in the upper right corner of the Visor screen and enter your classes.

2. Tap New assignment icon (on the icon bar).

3. Tap the Details icon and enter the information about the assignment including class, type, when due (both date and time), a description, number of points the assignment is worth, and the assignment's weight.

4. Tap OK.

N O T E   The documentation that accompanies Due Yesterday is just full of terrific ideas for managing grades and does everything but get you high grades without studying!

The following chart gives the key commands you'll need for Due Yesterday.

Menu	Command	Shortcut	What It Does
Action	**New Assignment**	**/N**	**Create a new assignment**
	Get Next Due	**/D**	**See nest due assignment**
	Get Class Grade	**/R**	**Get current class grade**
	Class Info	**/I**	**Get information on class**
Delete	**Assignment**	**/A**	**Delete an assignment**
	Class	**/L**	**Delete a class**
	Completed	**/O**	**Mark a class as competed**
Edit	**Undo**	**/U**	**Undo last action**
	Cut	**/X**	**Cut information**
	Copy	**/C**	**Copy information**

Menu	Command	Shortcut	What It Does
Edit	Paste	/P	Pastes information
	Select All	/S	Selects all information
	Keyboard	/K	Uses the keyboard to enter information
	Graffiti	/G	Uses Graffiti to enter information
Options	Font	/F	Select a font
	List	/T	Select listing options
	About	/B	All about Due Yesterday

Healthy Mind, Healthy Body

It's time to bulk up and get in shape, all with the help of your Visor. You can't watch a Tai Bo session on your Visor screen, but you can track your daily activity in great detail with the Athlete's Diary and even your consumption of junk food after the workout.

The sample of Visor applications explained here is varied, fun, and easy to use. But this is only the tip of the iceberg. On the accompanying disk and on the Internet, you can find thousands of programs covering every sport from swimming to soccer to luge.

Now get out there and give me 20 jumping jacks!

59 Your Visor Is Your Personal Trainer: Exercise

Exercise, Version 2

www.smasher.com/Palm/exercise.html

Freeware

What a good idea! Now when you exercise you can use Exercise, a specialized counter that allows you to count the number of repetitions and such associated with your pushups, sit-ups, or weight reps.

For each of nine exercises, Exercise can store the following information:

- ◆ The name of the exercise
- ◆ The number of reps (1-99) you want to do
- ◆ The time (1-99 seconds) each rep will take
- ◆ Support for up to 32 exercises in 7 routines
- ◆ If you do the exercise once or twice (right/left)
- ◆ If you want Exercise to beep $1/4$, $1/2$, and $3/4$ of the way through a set

Getting Started with Exercise

All Exercise entries are timed for 20 repetitions, four seconds apart. Here's how to create a new one:

1. Tap the number of the exercise you want to count for (1 through 9).

2. Tap the Start button.

To create a new exercise, follow these steps:

1. Tap the Edit button.

2. Enter a name for the exercise.

3. Enter the number of repetitions you want to do.

4. Enter the amount of time you want between each exercise.

5. Tap the Save button and you're in business.

60 Keep Track of Your Workouts: The Athlete's Diary

The Athlete's Diary, Version 1.0.8

www.stevenscreek.com/pilot/dodownload.html

Shareware: $39.95

Whether you swim, bike, or run, this is the program that will help you track everything from where you ran that beautiful sunny day in May to how fast you swam on the opening day of the long course season. This very user-friendly Visor application has the following features:

◆ Pre-designed for swimming, biking, and running (especially for tri-athletes)

◆ Allows for the creation of new sports

◆ Specification of yards, meters, miles, kilometers, and conversion of one to the other

◆ Free-form entry of notes about a workout

◆ Autofill of regularly entered data (such as running routes)

◆ Keywords entered using a pop-up menu

◆ Totals and graphs display numbers of workouts, time, and distance for any sport, and also any other numerical quantity such as weight, heart rate, or ascent

◆ Daily, weekly, and total views

◆ Graphing capabilities

If you're serious about tracking your training, The Athlete's Diary is the way to go.

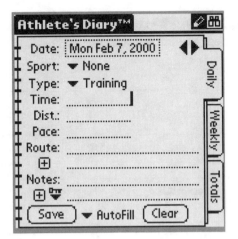

Getting Started with The Athlete's Diary

To record a workout, follow these steps:

1. Enter the date in the Date field.

2. Use the pop-up menu to select a sport.

3. Enter the distance and time. The Athlete's Diary will then compute the pace (distance divided by time).

4. Enter your route or use a keyword to assist you.

5. Enter notes or use a keyword to assist you.

6. Tap Save.

The chart below will help you get familiar with The Athlete's Diary.

Menu	Command	Shortcut	What It Does
Options	Purge Records	None	Purges all records based on date or duplicates
	About TAD	None	All about TAD
Edit	Undo	/U	Undoes the last operation

Menu	Command	Shortcut	What It Does
Edit	Cut	/C	Cuts information and places it on the clipboard
	Copy	/X	Copies information and places it on the clipboard
	Paste	/P	Pastes information from the clipboard
	Select All	/S	Selects all the information in a record
	Keyboard	/K	To use the keyboard to enter data
	Graffiti	/G	To use graffiti to enter data

61 Your Visor Is Your Diet Counselor: Food Counter

Food Counter, Version 1.0d

www1.Palmgear.com/software/showsoftware.cfm?prodID=3126

Freeware

You can try the grapefruit diet, the carbo-addicts diet, the all eggs, meat, butter, and cheese diet, or the Slim-Body diet, but none have any lasting effects. Want to lose weight? Eat right and exercise. That works. But if you plan on eating right and reducing both calories and fat, you'd better know what you're eating. The JFile add on, Food Counter, provides you with a database of 696 foods and contains the values for each item in the following categories:

- ◆ calories (CAL)
- ◆ protein (PR)
- ◆ carbohydrates (CAR)
- ◆ fat (F)

DB: FoodPro ▶				
ITEM	**CAL**	**PR**	**CAR**	**F**
Apple C'berry j	80	0	19	0
Apple Juice 8 o	116	0.2	29	0.
Apricot Nectar	141	0.9	36	0.
Cappuccino 6 o	64	0.6	10.4	2.
Carrot Juice 8	96	2.5	22	0
Coffee brewed	3	0	0.3	0
Cola 12 oz.	162	0	37.5	0
Cola diet 12 oz.	1	0	0.4	0
Cranberry Juic	147	0.1	38	0.
Ginger Ale 12 o	113	0	29	0

[Done] [Add] [Find] [+] [Del]

To make using Food Counter even easier, foods are categorized under major headers. You can sort items, filter them, find them, and add your own. So if you want to find a treat that's especially low in calories, you can sort in descending order by calories; you'll probably end up with a nice, delicious glass of water (with 0 calories). Food Counter is a great way to track your caloric and fat intake.

NOTE Like many databases, they need database programs to use them. You already know about HanDbase; Food Counter uses JFile, available at http://www.land-j.com/. Once again, it's a database application with loads of applications designed especially for it.

Getting Started with Food Counter

To locate a food you want to know the dietary numbers for, follow these steps:

1. Tap the Find button.

2. Enter the name of the item you want to find.

3. Tap the Find It button.

To find nutritional data on any other kind of food, just scroll down the list until you find the food you are looking for. The following chart shows the major commands for Food Counter.

Menu	Command	Shortcut	What It Does
Options	Apps Pref	/P	JFile preferences
	Database Prefs	/B	JFile preferences
Tools	Sort Items	/S	Sorts foods by name, calories, protein, carbohydrates, and fat in ascending or descending order
	Filter Records	/F	Filters foods by any variable
	Advanced Filter	/V	Filters foods by combination of variables
	Show All Records	/L	Shows all the records in the database
	Delete All Records	/D	Deletes all records
	Delete Filtered Recs.	/I	Deletes only filtered records
	Show 'Hidden' Columns	/H	Shows hidden columns

Menu	Command	Shortcut	What It Does
Tools	Print Records	/N	Prints records
	New Record	/R	Creates a new record
	Goto Top of DB	/T	Goes to the top of the database
	Goto Bottom of DB	/O	Goes to the bottom of the database
	Goto First Field	/Y	Jumps a certain number of records
	Goto Last Field	/Z	Removes all records from the database
Help	About JFile	/A	All about JFile

62 Determine When Your Baby Will Be Born: PregCalc

PregCalc, Version 3.2

www.thenar.com

Shareware: $20

Many people certainly hope they won't need this program, but if your time has come, you really want to know when the nursery should be ready.

PregCalc does the simple but important job of estimating the date of birth given the beginning of the women's last menstrual cycle. This is not exactly the precision of physics (as almost anyone who has had a baby will tell you), but it does give you a general guideline as to when you can expect the blessed event to happen and when you should have that bag packed.

What does PregCalc do (get out your medical text)? It calculates the following:

◆ EDD from LMP

◆ LMP from EDD

◆ Gestational age on any given date

◆ Gestational age from ultrasound data

◆ Mean fetal measurements for a given gestational age

◆ Can save and recall patient data (new to the professional version)

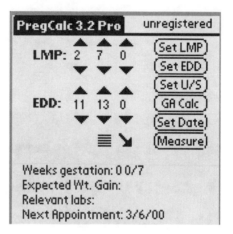

WARNING Major warning Will Robinson! Don't rely upon the results of this program to make your reservations at the hospital or call the grandparents! This is only an approximation and while it may be a very good one, new babies come both early and late and there are far too many factors to account for to predict with any accuracy when they will come.

Getting Started with Pregcalc

To use PregCalc, follow these steps:

1. Tap LMP (for first day of last menstrual period) or EDD (for expected date of delivery) and you will see a calendar to set the date of the event. PregCal will then compute the other variable (EDD if you entered LMP or LMP if you entered EDD). For convenience, you can also click today as the LMP or EDD.

2. If you have the information, set the U/S variable which represents the date of an ultrasound procedure.

3. Enter the gestational age in weeks and days as determined by the ultrasound (from the technician or your doctor).

4. Tap OK and the EDD will be adjusted given that information.

There are just a couple of commands for PalmPrint, and they are shown in the following chart.

Menu	Command	Shortcut	What It Does
Options	About PregCalc	/A	All about PregCalc
	Register	/R	Register PregCalc
	HotSync Name?	/H	Assigns same name as used to Hot Sync
Patients	Store Patients	/S	Store patient data
Edit	List Patients	/L	Lists patient data
	Delete Patient	/D	Deletes patient data

NOTE You can also adjust the LMP (last menstrual period) or EDD (expected due date) settings using the up and down arrows above the dates and also see the expected weight gain for the mom.

63 Keep Track of What Your Child Needs: TealInfo Immunization Guide

TealInfo Immunization Guide, Version 1.56

www.tealpoint.com

Shareware: $16.95

It's always confusing as to when a child should receive his or her next immunization. This excellent program not only tells you when and for what, but also about possible complications, what you need when you travel, and contraindications regarding the vaccine. This is a complete immunization guide with information on the 1999 American Association of Pediatrics immunization schedule. Here are the diseases that are covered:

♦ Rotasheild

♦ Hepatitis B

♦ DtaP

♦ Polio

♦ Hib

♦ MMR

♦ Varicella

Other nice features include:

♦ A guide for children over and under 7 years of age who missed some shots

♦ Specific information about hepatitis, Lyme Disease, and influenza vaccines

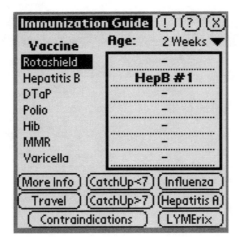

NOTE The Immunization Guide requires that you have TealInfo installed. You can find it on the companion CD.

Getting Started with TealInfo Immunization Guide

Tap the ▼ arrow for information about the particular age of the child to be immunized. The type of immunization needed will be shown. The chart below shows the commands you will need for the program.

Menu	Option	Shortcut	What It Does
Info	About TealInfo	/A	About TealInfo Immunization Guide
	Register	/R	How to register
	Help	/H	Help on TealInfo Immunization Guide
	Preferences	/P	Alphabetizes lists

Menu	Option	Shortcut	What It Does
Info	Details	/E	Backup HotSync
	Close	/X	Close TealInfo Immunization Guide

Your
Traveling
Guide

Almost everyone who owns a Visor takes it with them when they travel, so it's no surprise that there are hundreds of travel-related programs that can make your life as a tourist, or a road warrior, much easier.

Gulliver does just about everything you want from tracking your flight information to the time you have to pick up your rental car. And once you get there, if you don't know the difference between a dinar, a shekel, and a franc, try one of the many currency converters that are available. Just don't forget those extra batteries.

64 Take Me With You When You Travel: Abroad

Abroad! Version 4.9

`www.geocities.com/SiliconValley/Peaks/9768/`

Shareware: $20

Abroad! is like having a native at your side, whether you're in the south of France or the Australian outback. With its four modules, including Currency Exchange, Unit Conversion, World Clock, and Country Information Database, you'll know how much money you have in your pocket, what it's worth, what time it is, and the capital of where you are! In addition, Abroad! has a comprehensive and informative Web-based manual (that only covers up to version 4.6 however), meaning that updates from the author can easily keep pace with any new version release. The Country Information Database contains information for over 260 countries and territories around the world. It also includes every country's location on the world map, the nation's capital city, currency (code and name), time (current time, variation from GMT, DST period), and local telephone information (country code, area code of capital, international dialing prefix). The opening screen offers you a choice of start-up views (such as World Click or Menu). And to make things even easier, you can use the find function to search on a country name, country code, capital, and/or international dialing codes. A set of opening screen options also allows you to customize

Abroad! based on your own travel needs and practices. This is a must-have, even if you're visiting a county you *think* you know.

Getting Started with Abroad!

Follow these steps to get moving with Abroad! and learn how to convert money:

1. Tap the $ icon on the opening screen.

2. Enter the value of the money you want converted into the local denomination.

3. Using the ▼ arrow, select the currency into which you want your entry converted.

The table below shows a list of the commands you'll need for Abroad!

Menu	Option	What It Does
Options	Edit Memo	Allows you to edit an attached memo
	Prefs	Allows you to set preference such as opening screen characteristics, time zone, and home currency settings
	About Abroad!	All about Abroad!

65 Convert to EEC Currency: EURO.calc

EURO.calc, Version 1.32

www.klaus.de

Shareware: $10

Visiting the newly organized European Union? Want to convert francs to euros? Euros to liras? When you use EURO.calc, you can convert between the new euro and all member currencies plus the United States dollar. And should you find it necessary, you can even create your own conversions. Pull-down menus allow you to quickly change between currencies. Selecting the input currency is done through the use of easy-to-reach pull-down menus. And if you really get into trouble over how many Euros that half-dozen croissants should cost, try the simple calculator—it can add, subtract, multiply, divide, and perform percentage calculations.

Getting Started with EURO.calc

Follow these steps:

1. Using the numbered keys, enter the number of euros you want to convert.

2. Click the ▼ arrow to select the currency you would like the euros table converted to. You can do this again with another down arrow (there are two conversions on the screen).

3. To select the input currency, tap on the triangle to open a pop-up menu or tap on the small black rectangle above the triangle to open a map of Europe, then tap on the desired country. Very cool.

Follow the commands in this chart to use EURO.calc.

NOTE Have no fear about today's screwy economy. EURO.calc lets you change the exchange rates so you know exactly what you are giving up and getting. See the options menu below for more information.

Menu	Option	Shortcut	What It Does
Edit	Copy	/C	Copies entries
	Paste	/P	Pastes entries
Options	EURO Exchange Rates: Table	None	Displays current exchange rates in a table
	EURO Exchange Rates: Map	None	Displays current exchange rates as maps
	Currencies	None	Allows user to set exchange rates

Menu	Option	Shortcut	What It Does
Options	Preferences	None	Allows user to set layout of keys, type of key (round edges, square, shadow, etc.), and use sound effects
About	Registration	None	How to register EURO.calc
	About PalmWIN	None	Information about the object-oriented library used to help create EURO.calc
	About EURO.calc	None	Information about EURO.cacl

66 Manage Your Frequent Flyer Miles: AirMiles

AirMiles, Version 1.05

www.handshigh.com/html/airmiles.html

Commercial software: $29.95

Remember the last time you traveled and you said to yourself, "Next time I'll record those miles and get that free trip to Spain." Well, don't leave it to the airline to do it for you. If they don't care about your luggage, they certainly don't care about giving you free trips. AirMiles helps you manage your frequent flyer miles and tracks all your miles for multiple freebie or incentive programs and quickly reports on the miles and awards you have earned. It also helps you track other bonuses such as miles for lodging or car rentals, boats, trains, and whatever else you use to get around.

AirMiles Edit

Type: ▼ Flight
Program: ▼ AAdvantage
Date: Sun 2/20/00
Miles: 344   Segs: 1
Bonus:
Expires: ☑ 3   years
Descr.:   To Indy for David!   ▼

(Done) (Delete...) (Note...)

Getting Started with AirMiles

To record air miles for a trip, follow these steps:

1. Tap the New button.

2. Select the carrier for which you are getting miles (such as air travel, rental car, lodging, etc.) or create a new one.

3. Select the specific program if you have one (such as AAdvantage).

4. Enter the date and number of miles traveled.

5. Enter the expiration date (check with the airline) and any description you may want as a note. A nice little record is kept of all your trips, including an icon representing the category for which the miles have been counted. Cute.

Some tips:

◆ Tap on the entry in the summary screen to edit the details of any award.

◆ To enter your own program, tap the ▼ arrow, then enter a new budget.

◆ Tap Note to add a note to any entry.

Refer to the following table to find the commands for AirMiles.

Menu	Command	Shortcut	What It Does
Options	Preferences	/S	Allows you to define how you want the date to appear
	Reconcile	/R	Checks off those awards that have been verified by the airline
	Export	/E	Exports to MemoPad (perfect for expense reports)
	Edit Programs	/G	Edits list of award programs
	About AirMiles	None	All about AirMiles
Reports	Mileage Report	/M	Computes miles for all flights
	Flight Report	/F	Summarizes overall flight information

67 Meet Your Travel Assistant: Gulliver

Gulliver, Version 1

www.landware.com

Commercial software: $39.95

Gulliver is your all-around travel assistant. He helps you keep track of just about anything related to that next trip (whether to the coast, or to Laputa, or the land of the Houyhnhnms), including hotel confirmation numbers, phone numbers, flight schedules, frequent flyer ID numbers, and other customizable information. Itinerary details are entered and from there, Gulliver summarizes your air, car rental, and sleeping arrangements in one handy screen where you can select any part of the trip for editing. Gulliver even has auto completing fields, several databases full of city and accommodation information, pop up menus, and a complete database of travel vendor phone numbers. What more could you ask for?

Rental Car Reservation

Vendor:	
Pick up:	Wed 2/9/00
Where:	
Return:	Thu 2/10/00
Where:	
Phone:	
Fax:	
Cost:	▼ Per day
Conf #:	

(Done) (Details) (Note) (New)

Getting Started with Gulliver

To create a new trip itinerary, follow these steps:

1. Tap the New button at the bottom of the Gulliver Trips screen.

2. Enter a trip title.

3. Enter the dates of travel.

4. Enter a purpose for the trip.

5. Enter a trip reference number or numbers (especially handy for the new no-paper electronic tickets).

6. Select a category.

7. Enter any additional notes you might want.

8. Tap Done and the trip becomes part of the larger itinerary.

You can now tap on any part of the trip itinerary to edit that part and you can add new elements of the trip or the overall itinerary using special screens for flight details, hotels, and rental car reservations. You can then view trips by category, title, or date, edit city information (to include airport symbols and time zones), and more. Very handy! The commands for

Gulliver appear in this table. These are commands for a flight, but they are similar to those for a car rental or a hotel accommodation.

Menu	Command	Shortcut	What It Does
Record	New Flight	/F	Enters a new flight reservation
	Delete Flight	/D	Deletes a flight
Edit	Undo	/U	Undoes most recent operation
	Copy	/X	Copies information
	Cut	/C	Removes information
	Paste	/P	Pastes information
	Select All	/A	Selects all information
	Keyboard	/K	Uses the keyboard to enter information
	Graffiti	/G	Uses Graffiti to enter information
Options	Help	None	Help on Gulliver
	Preferences	/R	To specify preferences for airlines, car rentals, or hotels
	About Gulliver	None	All about Gulliver

68 Keep Tabs on Road Trips: Highway Manager Pro

Highway Manager Pro, Version 2.54

www.zorglub.com/pilot/highway/highway.html

Shareware: $12.95

I don't know how these Visor programmers did it! For $12.95, you can get a data manager that takes care of just about anything regarding gas and your car. Take a look at these features:

◆ Support for metric or Imperial (that's U.S.) measures

◆ Conversions for up to 10 currencies

◆ Absolute and relative distances

◆ Trips

◆ Accurate trip calculations

◆ Multiple vehicles

◆ Notes

◆ Fast data entry

◆ Display of ownership

◆ Data export via MemoPad

So if you want to know how much gas you used from L.A. to N.Y. (or Pisa to Rome), how many miles you got per gallon, and also make a note about the best hamburger joint on I-70, Highway Manager Pro can do it easily and quickly.

```
┌─────────────────────────────────────┐
│ Highway Manager ▼ Car 1             │
│ ▼ All Trips  (New) Start: 0         │
│ Date Miles  Gal.   Cur  Amt         │
│ 2/7   332   11.20  USD  15.34       │
│ 2/9   234   10.00  USD  13.24       │
│                                     │
│                                     │
│ G/100:   6.38    🗎 🎿 i 🗑          │
│ Amt/100: 8.60    Miles:   332       │
│ Mi/G:   15.66    Amount: 28.58      │
└─────────────────────────────────────┘
```

Getting Started with Highway Manager Pro

Follow these steps to use Highway Manager Pro:

1. Tap the New button on the opening screen.

2. Enter a date different from today if necessary (you can tap on the date and use the calendar).

3. Enter the number of miles traveled.

4. Enter the amount of gas used.

5. Enter the amount spent on the gas.

6. Tap the screen and you'll see the various statistics regarding gas usage.

The commands for Highway Manager Pro are shown in this table.

Menu	Option	Shortcut	What It Does
Record	New	/N	Creates a new entry
	Single Entry Stats	/I	Examines the information for a single entry

Menu	Option	Shortcut	What It Does
Record	Data Range Stats	None	Examines entries within a certain range of dates
	All Vehicle Stats	None	Finds out the information for all vehicles
	Add/Edit note	/O	Adds or edits a note
	Delete Item	/D	Deletes the active item
	Delete/Compact Range	None	Deletes a range of items by date
	Sort	/S	Sorts items by date, mileage, gallons, etc.
	Export Vehicle	None	Exports information
Edit	Keyboard	/K	Uses the keyboard to enter information
	Graffiti	/G	Uses Graffiti to enter information
Options	Edit Currencies	/C	Edits the currency being used
	Edit Trip	/T	Edits information about a particular trip
	Edit Vehicles	/V	Edits information about a particular vehicle
	Edit Categories	/E	Edits categories use for classifying trips
	Preferences	/P	Defines units of gas use, currency, and the way decimals are displayed

Menu	Option	Shortcut	What It Does
Help	About...	/A	All about Highway Manager Pro
	Register	None	Registers Highway Manager Pro
	Show HotSync ID	None	Shows your Id for HotSync-ing

69 What You Want to Know About L.A.: CitySync

CitySync from Lonely Planet

www.citysync.com

Commercial software: $19.95

The set of Lonely Planet CitySync cities includes a detailed and very informative set of maps, guides, and whatever else you need to know to find your way around town and have a good time. So far, they have guides to San Francisco, Las Vegas, Paris, Sydney, and coming soon are New York, Hong Kong, London, Chicago, Miami, Los Angeles, New Orleans, and Bangkok.

Learn about restaurants, clubs, shopping, and more, and add your own travel notes and even bookmarks.

70 Navigating The Unfriendly Skies: A Consumer Guide to Air Travel

A Consumer Guide to Air Travel

www.coslink.net/PalmaSrv

Document/Add-In Software (you need the iSilo reader)

Want to know *all* about overbooking? How about your rights concerning cancelled flights, or travel scam (more popular then ever). And then there's the contract (yes, your ticket is actually a contract) – want to know what it says? Pretty scary, huh?

A Consumer Guide to Air Travel will take you through these topics and the following and help make those skies a bit friendlier for you. This is good material to read well before you take a trip, and even carry it with you so that when the ill-informed flight attendant says you must hold your child on takeoff, you can show that person the real rules.

- ◆ Air Fares
- ◆ Reservation and Tickets
- ◆ Delayed and Canceled Flights
- ◆ Overbooking
- ◆ Baggage
- ◆ Smoking
- ◆ Passengers with Disabilities

- ◆ Frequent Flyer Programs
- ◆ Contract Terms
- ◆ Travel Scams
- ◆ Your Health
- ◆ Airline Safety
- ◆ Complaining

Getting Started with A Consumer Guide to Air Travel

A Consumer Guide to Air Travel is an iSilo document add-in. This means you need the iSilo reader, which you can get on the CD or at www.isilo.com for free. Once the reader is installed, the guide will show up on the opening iSilo menu.

Too Cool for Words

The title of this section says it all. This is where the Visor really lets loose and shows you what the imagination of some very creative programmers can come up with—from a piano complete with several octaves to recipes for tonight's dinner to your very own psychoanalyst. And on any of the web sites where you can get all these Visor programs, the fun/miscellaneous section usually has the largest selection – says something, right?

The material in this section, while not as practical in some ways as others presented throughout the book, does show a side to the Visor that illustrates its very best qualities as a tool that can just about fit the ideas and personality of any user. Be sure to check out the applications on the accompanying CD-ROM; you're sure to enjoy them.

A Stylus for Everyone

Everyone is trying to get on the bandwagon of selling things that you can use with your Visor, and there's a very nice selection from which to choose. What follows is a brief description of the some of the best that have been absolutely field-tested by the IDKYCDT Consumer Protection Division (a.k.a. your loyal author).

These are all good useful products that enhance the use of your Visor and worth a close look.

Your Visor comes with a plastic stylus that is about as unfashionable and poorly designed as the Visor is fashionable and very nicely designed. So, it's no wonder that there are a few companies now creating styli (yes, that's the plural of stylus) for use with your Visor.

PDA Panache (www.pdapanahce.com) has been in business since the early days of the PalmPilot and is now designing styli for the Visor. They offer many different models from the simple Stick Stylus (only a $1.95) which is nothing more than a plastic stick with a writing tip (but very useful in quantity, especially with your company logo) to the classy Deluxe Stylus which comes in gold, black, or sliver. This metal stylus is hefty enough so that you feel like there's something in your hand but small enough to fit in the Visor holder. Then you can move up to the Stylus/Pen/Pencil combo that includes all three – just a click of a button selects the one you want. Such a stylus is about the size of a fountain pen and very handy if you switch from paper to your Visor. You can find refills at the PDA Panache site for all their products.

What's especially attractive about the company is their 30-day money back satisfaction guarantee and their lifetime writing tip replacement offer. If you wear out the writing tip (hello Superman), they'll repair it and return it to you at no charge.

Pilot Pen Corporation of America (`www.pentopia.com`) also offers an outstanding collection of styli for the Visor user. Especially nice is the Chameleon Neon line that are small plastic styli with a writing tip on one end and a ballpoint pen on the other. These were originally designed for the PalmPilot and are just a hair too small for the Visor, but still can be used. Just be careful not to push it down too far into the stylus holder slot on your Visor.

Pilot also offers a stylish multi-function stylus that includes a stylus, a ballpoint pen, and a mechanical pencil (like the PDA Panache model). All the Pilot styli are guaranteed for one year.

Keeping a Very Clean and Fit Machine

I'll bet you're the same way. You absolutely can't stand it when someone puts a big greasy finger on your Visor screen and it's there to stare you in the face until you have a chance to clean it up.

Well, you might want to use a very diluted and gentle window cleaner or a bit of vinegar and water, but you can also turn to ConceptKitchen (`www.conceptkitchen.com`) for not only cleaning accessories, but other products that will keep your Visor humming away.

First, let's do the cleaning. Try (the small enough to fit in your Visor case) Karma Cloth to remove fingerprints and oils and keep the screen shiny and clear. This small red soft cloth delivers lint free cleaning. But, if you need a major cleaning, try The PDA Screen Clean™ which includes Brain Wash. Brain Wash consists of a pre-moistened towelette that you use to clean your screen, and then a soft lint free cloth to dry it off. Since you'll never use the entire cloth's surface to clean and shine your Visor, now's a good time to clean your monitor screen as well!

The next level of protection is to use one of the WriteRights. Concept Kitchen claims than this is the top-selling PDA accessory in the world, and they might very well be right. This is a thin, clear sheet of plastic that adheres to the Visor screen and allows protection from scratches as well as a more textured surface on which to write. In other words, your handwriting recognition might improve since there's less slipping on the screen and perhaps your Visor will see your scribblings as being more accurate. The WriteRight sheets take a bit of practice to get used to putting on, but they are easily removed if you need to reposition one.

The WriteRight, Brain Wash and Karma Cloth come as part of the PDA Survival Kit; just the present for the Visor owner you know and love. In addition to the above, the Survival Kit also comes with a set of PenCap Sylus'. These fingernail looking, clear styli, replace the cap of your favorite disposable pen and are terrific substitutes for any of the styli we've already mentioned. They allow you to use that pen as a pen, or just attach the FingerTip to the other end or even use it as the cap. And the designers of these Finger-Tip Styli had the right idea – many people, especially those with long-index finger nails, use those nicely manicured nails as the stylus – just think, it's always there when you need it and can virtually never be lost.

There are many other accessories for your Visor from Coach leather cases to specialized holders for your car. The best way to find out about them is to visit the web sites we mention in Appendix A, where most commercial companies advertise or have their product reviewed.

71 Just Dial 698-4767: Vanity

Vanity, Version 1

www.concepts.de

Freeware

Ever wonder how all those Madison Avenue types think up those catchy 1-800 numbers with the cute phrases to accompany them? Wonder no longer. Although their home page is in German (Oy!), this program is a cinch to use and lots of fun. You enter the words you want such as Go Hawks (for the benefit of University of Kansas basketball fans) or GeorgeW (for you know who) and the program converts the characters into the correct numerals.

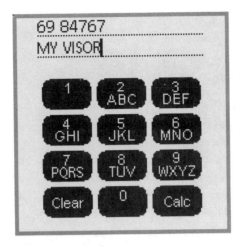

Getting Started with Vanity

The main Vanity screen looks like a typical keypad with letters and accompanying numbers. To get Vanity to produce those vanity license plates or winning home phone number, follow these steps:

1. Enter your characters for which you want corresponding numbers.

2. Tap the Calc button (just like you would on a calculator) and the corresponding characters appear at the top of the screen as you see in the figure.

3. Tap the Clear button to start over.

Having fun yet? Here are some Vanity 1-800 numbers for our aspiring presidential candidates.

Bill Bradley 1-800-244-2455 (BigBill)

Al Gore 1-800-877-3725 (VpresAL)

George W. Bush Jr. 1-800-436-7439 (GeorgeW)

John McCain 1-800-843-8838 (VietVet)

Steve Forbes 1-800-742-4489 (RichGuy)

72 Play Piano: Palm Piano

Palm Piano, Version 1.0

`www.snafu.de/~tjawer/tjhome.htm`

Shareware: $5

You're probably not playing at Carnegie Hall but you can play some piano music with the best of them using PalmPiano. With this 4-Octave piano program, you can create your own melody—up to 1000 notes long. Then, save it and recall it for your next round of inspiration.

Getting Started with Palm Piano

Follow these steps:

1. To record a song, tap Record and then tap the keys in the song.

2. To stop recording, tap StpRec.

3. To pause while recording, tap the Pause button.

4. To delete a song, tap the Delete button.

5. To go to the beginning of a song, tap the B button.

6. To go back one note and hear a song, tap the < button.

7. And to play your magnum opus, tap the Play button.

This Table will get you familiar with the commands in Palm Piano.

Menu	Command	Shortcut	What It Does
Auswahl	Info	/I	Information about Visor Piano
	How To Use	/U	Tips on how to use Visor Piano
	How To Register	/R	How to register Visor Piano

And here's what all the buttons in Palm Piano do:

Delete: Deletes the whole song

B: Go to the beginning of the recorded song

E: Go to the end of the recorded Song

<: Go one note backward and hear it

<: Go one note forward and hear it

Play: Play the recorded song

Rest: In record mode you can insert a pause (Rest)

StpRec: With this button, you can stop the record –mode

73 Answer the Questions of the Universe: Yoda

Yoda, Version 1

http://www1.Palmgear.com/software/Freeware

Seeking inspiration? Guidance? Answers to the universe's most puzzling questions such as, "Where are my keys?" Find it here, from Yoda, the Jedi master who will guide you to wisdom.

Getting Started with Yoda

You tap whether you want Yoda to give you wisdom or answers and it's there in a Tatooine second. This Visor application won't conquer the dark side, but it sure is fun.

74 Visit a Psychologist: Eliza, Visor Psychologist

Eliza, Visor Psychologist, Version 1

www.ddhsoftware.com

Freeware

Now note this first. This is just for fun and is not meant to replace therapy or the use of other professionals to cure your ills. No kidding.

That said, this is a terrifically cool application—and one that is lots of fun. It mimics more powerful applications that use artificial intelligence—you tell Dr. Eliza your problems or concerns, and she responds, setting up an ongoing transaction between you and your Visor, err—Eliza. So, what to do about all those applications? Here's the free advice Eliza gave me:

> Me: I seem to have this need to add more and more applications onto my Visor. Can you help?

> Eliza (as most good therapists do) comes back with a question of her own: "Don't you believe I can help?"

> Me: Of course.

> Eliza: Neil, do you have any psychological problems?

> Me: How would I know? That's why I'm here!

Getting Started with Eliza

The main Eliza screen contains two fields. At the top are Eliza's words, and at the button are yours. There are also two buttons at the bottom labeled Tell Eliza and Clear. To work with Eliza (at the reduced rate of $0 per hour), follow these steps:

1. Enter your feelings and questions to Eliza using graffiti or the keyboard.

2. Tap the Tell Eliza button when you are finished. Eliza will respond to what you wrote, and the therapeutic process begins.

Follow these shortcuts to get in touch with your inner child.

Menu	Command	Shortcut	What It Does
File	New Session	/N	Time's up! Starts a new session
Edit	Cut	/X	Cuts text from Eliza
	Copy	/C	Copies text from Eliza
	Paste	/P	Pastes text into Eliza from another Visor application
	Keyboard	/K	To use the keyboard to enter text
About	About	/A	All about Eliza

75 Age-Old Game: Sticks

Sticks

www.beiks.com/palmzonebg/sticks.htm

Commercial software: $5

How's this for a quote from the homepage for Sticks? "Like most of the good things in the world (like sex and hot water), Sticks is fairly simple and yet truly addictive."

If that's not enough to pique your interest, it's time to move on. But, if you're ready for lots of fun and a truly addictive game experience, Sticks is it. The object is to clear the pile of sticks on the playing field and the higher the level of the game (of which there are 12 levels) the faster the sticks come and the more challenging the game becomes. This is like the old' pick up sticks game only all bulked up for action.

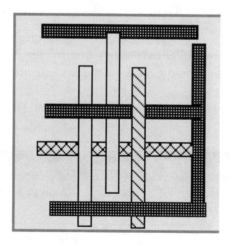

Getting Started with Sticks

Here's how to play this simple game:

1. Click on the top stick until all the sticks are removed.

The chart below shows the commands for Sticks.

Menu	Command	Shortcut	What It Does
Options	New Game	/N	Starts a new game
	Preferences	/P	Allows you select game preferences
	Registration	/R	Registers Sticks
	High Score	None	Shows high scores

76 If You Need to Know Where You Are: SoftGPS

SoftGPS

Shareware: $568 (no kidding!)

There's fun, and then there's *fun*. This Visor application really takes the cake. We won't tell you too much about it—you can sort of guess what it is when you look at the illustration that follows. But, if you have any friends with Visors who are hot shot pilots, geographers, or just plain old techies, tell them that this is an incredibly cool Geosynchronous Positioning System that doesn't need hardware like their expensive do-dads. Rather, this is all software driven – then let them try it and watch as they laugh and go nuts at the same time. Don't you love this stuff?

77 A Little Weird, but Fun: Cupidotron

Cupidotron

`perso.cybercable.fr/nucleus/pipotron/index.html` (in French)

Freeware

It's not everyday that you can crank up your Visor and get a load of words that seem a bit random in nature, but fun nonetheless. Put Cupidotron and its random declarations of love on your honey's Visor next Valentine's day and watch the fireworks start!

Getting Started with Cupidotron

There's not much to do other than tap the More! button to another witty collection of love notes or tap the Copy button to copy the notes into your MemoPad or any other application on your Visor.

Cupidotron ℹ️

My hairy teletuby,

You are like a star of polystyrene. I don't mind to caress you next weekend in an igloo.

Mad kisses from your stressed rocket launcher.

(Copy) (More!)

78 Hop to It: Kanga.ru

Kanga.ru, Version 1.1

www.palmgear.com/software/showsoftware.cfm?prod#=5955

Freeware

This is not your average game and it's too cool to be placed in the games category. Kanga.ru has terrific graphics, is fun and easy, yet can be challenging to play. The goal is to catch coconuts and the way you do that is by aiming the kangaroo and let it do the rest. If you miss, you lose one of your lives. If you make it, you increase your score.

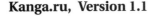

OK – we'll tell you – why the .ru? Because these folks will be starting a commercial web venture named, what else, but `www.kanga.ru`, which may even be live when you read this.

Getting Started with Kanga.ru

To play Kanga.ru with the stylus, tap the place near the kangaroo and it will turn to this direction. You can also play without tapping by placing the stylus on to the screen and moving it without lifting. See the table below for Kanga.ru's commands.

Menu	Command	Shortcut	What It Does
Help	Help	/H	Help
	About	/A	About Kanga.ru

79 eBay, Here We .Com: Auctioneer

Auctioneer, Version 1.2

`www.setocorp.com/products.htm`

Shareware: $10

It had to happen sooner or later. Now, in the middle of your meeting about whether the delivery trucks should be painted blue or gold, you can check your eBay auctions and see how much you want to bid on that BigBoy (now at $3,575) that you've wanted for years. All you need is a Visor modem and a connection to the Internet.

Auctioneer shows the item description, latest bids, the auction closing dates and times, and allows you to get the latest auction data using a wired or wireless modem connected to your Visor. Or, you can download the same information by Hotsyncing through the corresponding desktop application.

Auctioneer-eBay		
Item Desc	Bid	Ends
23544334	.00	

(Go WWW)   (New)

Getting Started with Auctioneer

The big steps in using auctioneer are adding items that it can then look for on eBay for the latest information. You cannot actually bid using Auctioneer. For that, you have to go to an Internet connection such as that provided by the Palm VII's service.

Here's how to add an auction item.

1. From the main screen, tap the "New" button. This brings up the New Item screen.

2. Enter eBay auction item numbers for items that you are interested in.

3. Tap OK.

Check out the table below for the commands needed for Auctioneer.

Menu	Command	Shortcut	What It Does
Option	Register	/R	Register Auctioneer
	About	/A	About Auctioneer

80 1st, 2nd and 3rd Degree: Alarms

Alarms

www.pedos.hr/~kdekanic/alarms.html

Shareware: $5

And all you thought the Visor could do was to wake you up with some wimpy beeping sound. How about the theme from the X-Files, Superman, Back to the Future, or Dr. Who? (you get the idea). This is one set of several available at this web site, which includes hundreds of different alarms you can use with your Visor. Want to know about more categories of alarms? There are

◆ games alarms

◆ cartoon alarms

◆ movie and TV alarms

◆ Christmas alarms

Mix and match them and drive the person at that meeting next to you completely nuts!

Getting Started with Alarms

To use the alarms, locate and download the set you want from the web site. Then, follow these steps:

1. HotSync the System_MIDI_Sounds.PDB file to your Visor device.

2. Tap and open the Datebook (where the alarms reside).

3. Tap Options>Preferences.

4. Tap the alarm you want to use.

81 Stuck Without a Milk Substitute: Cook's Companion

Cook's Companion, Version 1

`http://www2.palmgear.com/software`

Document Add-In

Here's a terrific recipe for French Silk Pie (and it makes two - one for you and the other for you too!)

1. Melt 8 ounces of unsweetened chocolate.

2. Cream 1 pound of butter and 3 cups of sugar.

3. Add 8 eggs and whip at high for three minutes.

4. Add melted chocolate in a stream while whipping.

5. Add to graham cracker pie shells and chill.

Out of granulated sugar? Use powdered or confectioner's. How much? Ah, we knew you would need to know. So, here's Cook's Companion, which provides you with a ton of cooking information. Cook's Companion is a quick reference guide for common measurement, temperature, and ingredient equivalents and substitutions. So if you want to know how many tablespoons are in a ¼ cup (4), or how may pounds are in a kilogram (2.2) or how many cups of whipped butter you get out of one pound (3)—look no further— this is it!

NOTE Cook's Companion is a document Add-in, so you need a document reader, and iSilo (also on the accompanying CD-ROM) works just fine.

```
▪ DAIRY

Butter, 1 stick
= 4 oz
= 8 tbs
= ¼ lb

Butter, 1 c
= 7/8 to 1 c shortening + ½ tsp salt
= 7/8 c lard + ½ tsp salt
= 1 c margarine

Butter, whipped, 1 lb
(Done) (Find)(Next)  ▼      (17%)
```

82 Guess What the BS Is For: BSBingo

BSBingo

`http://www.thisiscool.com`

Freeware

So you're in another one of those meetings and you're hoping that a natural disaster will occur to break the boredom. Well, not really, but you surely need a break. BSBingo to the absolute rescue. Every time someone uses one of the words in the left-hand list of words on the screen, you select it, which fills in a square on the bingo board. When you get bingo (five squares across, down, or diagonally) you win (and BSBingo flashes)! Of course, you can't really tell anyone, but what the hell – it's fun.

NOTE Want your own specialized list for BSBingo? Then you must really be looking for a new job. Anyway, you can create them as word lists in MemoPad with the first line of the memo starting with /@-BSBingo:<title> where <title?> is the list's name. Then add exactly 25 lines of words and use the menu command Game |Load Word List option. You'll see the list title and then just select it and bingo on!

Getting Started with BSBingo

Easy? You bet. Just tap the words as they're said and a square is filled. See the following chart for the commands.

Menu	Command	Shortcut	What It Does
Game	New Game	/N	Starts a new game
	Load Word List	/L	Loads a word list
	Options	/O	Allows you to change the message when you get bingo

Menu	Command	Shortcut	What It Does
Help	Instructions	/I	How to play BSBingo
	About	/A	All about BSBingo

83 So Much Fun: It's Useless

Useless, Version 1.5

`http://members.tripod.com/palmiiixcenter/`

Freeware

We're not going to show you a graphic of this screen; otherwise, we'd give away all the fun that it brings to your Visor. So once you download this application, be sure to tap the About button to learn all about the rock solid guarantee. It's worth the trouble. By the way, this application was created using Palm Factory Studio, in Visor: IDKYCDT!

84 Light Up!: EasyView

EasyView, Version 2

`www.palmix.itil.com`

Freeware

Some people love to use their backlight feature and some don't. For those who do, but also find it bothersome to hold down the start button for more than two seconds (Yikes!), there's EasyView. EasyView can be set to turn on the backlight feature and turn it off at clock times that you preset. Easy, fun and a time saver for those of you who *must* have your Visor light up at the perfect moment.

Getting Started with EasyView

Just follow these steps to set the time to light up your screen:

1. Specify the time periods during which you want the Auto-On feature active.

2. Save the time settings by tapping Save.

3. Tap the Activate button.

85 Confused by Trading Cards: The Finer Life Pokémon Guide

The Finer Life Pokémon Guide

www.duwa-prod.com

Shareware: $5

What? You didn't know that Charizard is a Lizard and that its element is Fire/Flying? Or that Butterfree is good in a battle against Grass and Psychic? Unless you're between 5 and 10 years old, don't feel bad. Instead, reach for the Finer Life database to see you through the Pokémon crisis in your own house. The Finer Life Pokémon Guide contains information on all 151 Pokémon including the Pokémon's attacks, how each one evolves, the Pokémon's strengths and weaknesses and information about height, weight, and Pokémon type. Now, isn't that better?

Database Item	
#:	10
English Name:	Caterpie
Japanese Name:	Caterpie
Attacks:	Tackle, String Shot
Evolution:	L07 Metapod L 10
	Butterfree
Element:	Bug
Pokémon Type:	Worm
Good Against:	Grass and Psychic
Bad Against:	Fire, Fighting, Flying, and Ghost

OK

Getting Started with the Pokémon Guide

To use the Finer Life Pokémon Guide, you need to download the Finer Life Database reader available at http://www.duwa-prod.com/databases.html (and on the CD-ROM that accompanies Visor!:IDKYCDT in the same folder as the Pokemon Guide). Then, just click on the character for which you want information.

NOTE The Finer Life Database Reader is much like HanDBase Teal, and JFile – they are specialized readers with their own set of database. Finer Life has about 30 such databases including cheese, restaurants, and cigars.

86 Track Peaks and Valleys: Biorhythms

Biorhythms, Version 1.5

www.jeffjetton.com

Shareware: $5

So today, you have to finish your taxes (mental), exercise (physical), and then apologize to your honey (Emotional) for being obnoxious (again). Is this the best day for either or all of these? Don't fret and don't consult your local psychic either. Why not use Biorhythms, which charts your physical, mental, and emotional state and lets you know the peaks and valleys.

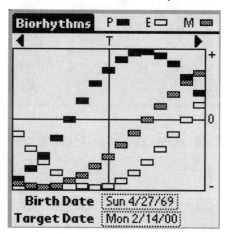

Getting Started with Biorhythms

To use Biorhythms, you need to provide your birth date:

1. Tap on the already entered Birth Date and you will see the Visor Calendar.

2. Set the new birth date and read the biorhythms for physical, mental, and emotional dimensions of life. Hare Krishna. If you were born before 1904, you're out of luck - Biorhythms only goes back that far.

This chart shows the main commands for Biorhythms.

Menu	Command	Shortcut	What It Does
Options	Birthdays	/B	List and save birthdays of your closest séance partners
	Exact Age	/E	Provides the exact age of the selected person
	About	/A	About Biorhythms
	Help	/H	Help

Hours of Fun: Games, Games, Games

True story. Your faithful author was at a concert and was pleased to see the concert goer next to him take out his Visor, figuring he was probably going to catch up on some business not finished during the days' work. Next thing I see, there's PacMan squirming around the screen and this frantic player trying to eat through all the dots! Fortunately, the lights went out and he had enough sense to turn on the backlight and continue.

If you like (or liked) Nintendo, Sega, Sega Dreamcast, Game Boy, or throwing quarters into arcade machines, you need read no further or pay attention to any other section of this book. Here, and on the companion CD-ROM, is just what you need for hours—if not days—of addictive, hypnotizing fun. And don't forget the Springboard modules by Visor (such as Tiger Woods which is now available) and others, which should be hitting the shelves by the time you read this book. May the force be with you.

87 Navigate a Spaceship through Enemy Territory: BombRun

BombRun, Version 1.

http://www.seimitsu.demon.co.uk/

Shareware: $8

Every collection of games has to have a "shoot-em-up", and this is mine. BombRun is an exciting space/shooting game. As pilot, your job is to fly a spaceship through enemy territory, avoiding the mountains and the bad guys, get to the enemy base, and then destroy it. You can change your flight speed, fire missiles, and move the ship up and down. Out of gas? Shoot an enemy fuel tank. This arcade-style game lets you track scores (for comparison's sake) as well as change the keyboard controls to better fit your preferences. The Options menu allows you to redefine or reassign keys and commands.

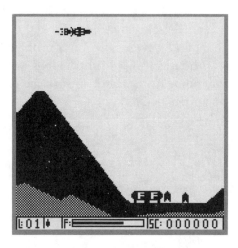

Getting Started with BombRun

To get going in BombRun, follow these steps:

1. Tap the Date/Calendar key to start a game.

2. Tap the Phone button to speed up.

3. Tap the Up and Down buttons to increase and decrease the height of the ship.

4. Tap the ToDo button to fire a missile.

5. Tap the Memo List button to pause. You can also tap and hold the Menu button to pause for as long as you tap.

88 Relive Your Frogger-Playing Youth: Frogs vs. Cars

Frogs vs. Cars, Version 1.02

`http://www.standalone.com`

Shareware $10

Frogger was (and still is) one of the classic arcade games that consumed thousands of adolescent's quarters during the 1980's. Now there's the Visor version—that may be even more fun. The object is to get the frog across the busy street without getting squished. Frogs vs. Cars records high scores so when you get home from school or work you can show your loved ones what you accomplished today.

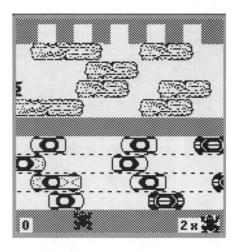

Getting Started with Frogs vs. Cars

Here's how you get started with Frogsvs. Cars:

1. The Date button moves the frog left.

2. The Phone button moves the frog up.

3. The Up button also moves the frog up.

4. The Down button moves the frog down.

5. The ToDo button also moves the frog down.

6. The Memo button moves the frog right.

Keep your froggy alive with the important commands shown in this Table.

Menu	Option	Shortcut	What It Does
Options	New Game	/N	Starts a new game
	Controls	None	Shows you which buttons control the frog's movement
	High Scores	None	Records players' high scores
	Enter Password	None	Allows you to enter a password once you have registered
	About Frogs vs. Cars	None	All about Frogs vs. Cars

89 The Truth is Out There: Galax

Galax, Version 1.1.e

www.pilotfan.com

Freeware

Along with Frogger, Galax is another of the all time great arcade machines. Remember all those quarters you invested in hours of fun with nothing to show when done? Well, Galax is a great arcade-style game in which your job is to get as many points killing as many aliens as you can. It's another shoot-em-up game that's more fun than BSBingo. Mr. Sulu! Warp 2!

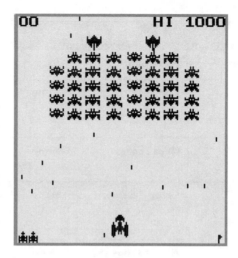

The various options before the game starts (selected using the Up button) are Start, Options (including reset high score, define shades - white, gray, or black), define keys, set Starfield (at high, medium, or off), and set volume. See the following table for the key commands.

Since this is a game controlled by Visor buttons, here's a summary of what buttons do what.

Button	Option	Shortcut	What It Does
Menu	Pause	None	Pauses the game
Calculator	Pause	None	Pauses the game
Notepad	Resume	None	Resumes the game
Day Book	Move to the right	None	Moves the ship to the right
Up	Move to the left	None	Moves ship to the left

90 Play PacMan on Your Visor: PacMan!

PacMan, Version 1.3

`http://Palm.pair.com`

Shareware: $10

If you just arrived from the planet Jupiter, you may not have heard of PacMan. This is the arcade game that drove millions of people stir crazy trying to figure out how to get all those little "packies" (Inky, Blinky, Pinky, and Clyde) eaten before they eat you. It's still one of the best around and it's almost a miracle that someone could program it to fit on that little Visor screen. The real miracle is that someone thought of this game in the first place!

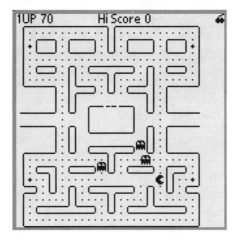

Getting Started with PacMan

Follow these steps to play PacMan:

1. To control the PacMan's movement, you can use the application and up/down buttons.

2. Tap the screen to change the direction of the creatures.

3. To start a new game without touching the screen, press the PageUp key and then the PageDown key in Game Over mode.

There are just a couple of important commands for PacMan, as shown below in this chart.

Menu	Option	Shortcut	What It Does
Game	New	/N	Starts a new game
	Hi-score	/H	Shows the high score
	About	/A	All about PacMan

91 Brush Up Your Chess Game: PocketChess

PocketChess, Version 1.1

http://www.eskimo.com/~scottlu

Shareware: $15

You might not ever be a Bobby Fisher or Gary Kasparov (or Big Blue for that matter), but that doesn't mean that you can't have a great time playing chess against your Visor. The version 1.1 release of PocketChess is a fully featured chess program. With a library of more than 80 opening moves and eight levels of difficulty, PocketChess will get and keep any chess player's attention.

The list of outstanding features for PocketChess is extensive and provides a realistic game environment for even intermediate and advanced players. Some of the best are:

◆ You can play against the game, against another human player, or even have your Visor play against another Visor!

◆ There are eight levels of difficulty to choose from.

◆ When you play, you are notified by a turn indicator, a last move indicator, and a last piece played indicator.

◆ There's a board setup mode to set up hypothetical chess positions and then play them.

◆ The Undo Move command undoes moves and remembers all moves back to the very first move.

◆ Need a hint? Use the /H keystroke command and have PocketChess make a suggested move. Don't like what the program did? Just undo it using the /U keystroke command.

◆ The Reverse Board command flips the board presentation.

◆ The chess game you are currently playing is always saved when you switch to another Visor application.

◆ Want something to pump up the match? Sound effects for check, checkmate, and pawn promotion are available. Want it quiet? Turn the sound off.

NOTE The developer of PocketChess is hard at work on version 2.0 and welcomes any feedback and suggestions from users. Now's your chance! Mail to scottlu@eskimo.com to share your ideas!

Getting Started with PocketChess

To use the various features that PocketChess offers, tap the Menu button on your Visor. See this table for key commands.

Menu	Command	Keystroke	What it does
PocketChess	New Game	/N	Starts a new game
	Setup Board	/S	To practice particular strategies, you can create and play specific board configurations
	Board Size	/B	Toggles between small and large board size
	Options	/O	Includes Skill Level, Sound Effects, and whether you want to play against your Visor, another player, or another Visor
	About	None	All about PocketChess

Menu	Command	Keystroke	What it does
Commands	Undo Move	/U	Undoes last move
	Hint	/H	Provides a hint as to what you could do next
	Skip	/M	Skips a player
	Reverse Board	/R	Reverses the pattern on the board
	Switch Sides	/W	Changes sides

92 21 or Bust: BlackJack Solitaire

BlackJack Solitaire, Version 1.2

http://www.seahorsesoft.com/

Shareware: $5

This will surely keep you engaged on that daily commute. The object of BlackJack Solitaire is to get the highest score for each row, without busting (going over 21 points for a row). And since the game is timed, there's an incentive to go *f-a-s-t*. Features? Lots— try these:

◆ You set the difficulty level, which in turn determines how much time each round has.

◆ The Practice round is just for fun and not timed.

◆ Each game is timed.

◆ There are four different levels of play.

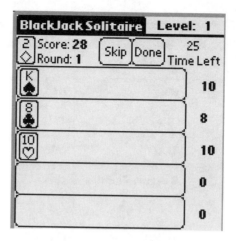

Getting Started with Blackjack

If you're not familiar with the card game, then start out with your Visor version of Blackjack somewhat slowly so you can get used to all the features and develop a strategy of your own. There are a total of three rounds played in a game and aces are automatically set to 1 or 11 depending on how that would affect the row. See the table that follows for the Blackjack's key commands.

Menu	Command	Shortcut	What It Does
Options	New Game	/N	Starts a new game
	Settings	/S	Changes the Blackjack difficulty and sound settings
	How To Register	/O	How to officially register
	Enter Code	/E	Enters the registration code

Menu	Command	Shortcut	What It Does
Stats	Best Scores	None	To see the best scores by level
	Ultimate Score	/U	To see the highest score
	Reset Scores	/R	To reset internally-kept scores
	Generate Code	/G	Generates entry-level codes
Rules	How To Play	/H	Instructions on how to play Blackjack
	About	None	All about Blackjack

93 Keep a Pair of Dice with You at All Times: Dice!

Dice, Version 1.0

http://www.quartus.net

Freeware

You just never know when a good game of Craps will come up—so why not be prepared? Dice! rolls two standard six-sided dice and is perfect for gamblers and game-players. No rocket science about this—it's just plain fun dice-throwing. Click and roll!

Getting Started with Dice

Tap the screen and watch the die change; that's all there is to it! Check out this chart for Dice's important commands.

Menu	Option	Shortcut	What It Does
Dice	Roll	/R	Rolls the two dice
Options	Help	/H	Help with Dice!
	About	/A	All About Dice!

94 The Ancient Classic: TetrisV

TetrisV

http://195.128.67.93

Shareware: $8

This is nothing short of a terrific game and one that was originally invented in the Soviet Union and imported around the world. It has many variants, but this is the original— based on the arcade success. If you load one game on to your Visor, this should be it. Features you ask? It's loaded:

- Very fast graphics
- See the next shape coming before it arrives
- Use extended figures
- Remap control buttons
- Statistics of your results
- Set garbage lines high or low
- Nine levels of speed
- Sound effects

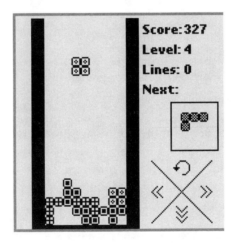

Getting Started with TetrisV

1. Tap the >> and << icons to move the shape to the left or right.

2. Tap the circular arrow icon to rotate the shape.

3. Tap the down arrows to move the shape quickly to the bottom of the screen.

Look at the following table for the commands you'll need for TetrisV.

Menu	Command	Shortcut	What It Does
Options	Keys	None	Remaps Visor keys
	Register	None	Register TetrisV
	About	None	All about TetrisV

95 Blow Your Cares Away: FanMate

FanMate, Version 2

`http://www.mobimate.com/index.html`

Freeware

Not in the mood for the oppressive humidity? Try this four-speed fan to blow away all your troubles. This is one of those fun applications that does nothing but amuse and it's worth the effort to download and surprise your other PalmPilot and Visor friends with. Uses very few batteries and never runs out of hot air.

What a Pretty Picture: Graphics and Design

Even if the picture is small, like on the screen of your Visor, it can still be worth a thousand words. You can read on your Visor, play games, even send e-mail to your honey—but you can also draw. Some of the creations using the applications you find here and on the companion disk are stunning. Just like you get to Carnegie Hall—it takes practice, practice, practice.

96 You Can Etch-a-Sketch but Don't Shake: Dinky Pad

Dinky Pad, Version .92b

`www.daggerware.com/dinkypad.htm`

Shareware: $5

Ever get that urge to just withdraw from a meeting and doodle? That's what's nice about DinkyPad. It's fast, easy to use, and your colleagues around the table will think that you're using some fancy spreadsheet to figure out the last quarter's gains while all the time you're doodling! But it's not just a scratch pad. This new improved version of Dinky Pad enables the following cool features:

- ◆ Multiple image files
- ◆ Use of thumbnail sketches from which you can select previous drawings
- ◆ Text notes attached to drawings
- ◆ Fewer jaggies!

N O T E Want some serious fun? Check out the DinkyPad Art Gallery at `http://www.daggerware.com/dinkyart.htm`.

Getting Started with DinkyPad

To create a graphic, follow these steps:

1. Tap the New button.

2. Select a drawing tool (such as open or the circle tool).

3. Draw the image you want.

See the following table for the commands you'll need for DinkyPad.

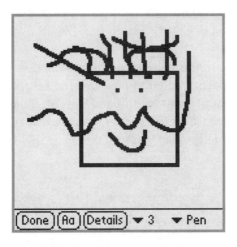

Menu	Command	Shortcut	What It Does
Record	**Top of Image**	**/T**	**Goes to the top of the image**
	Bottom of Image	**/B**	**Goes to the bottom of the image**
	Delete Record	**/D**	**Deletes both the image and text**
Edit	**Erase Screen**	**/E**	**Erases the current drawing but leaves the screen open**
Options	**About DinkyPad**	**/I**	**All about DinkyPad**

97 A Groovy Screen Saver for Your Visor: Magic Squares

Magic Squares, Version 1

`beta.homestead.com/htebeka/index.html`

Freeware

This Visor program doesn't do a lot, but it does do one thing very well: It displays cool animated squares on your Visor screen. This is not earth shaking, but perhaps soothing to stare at, much like those goldfish or toaster screensaver things that have been so popular. Besides, it's lots of fun—especially when you turn out all the lights in the room and backlight your Visor screen!

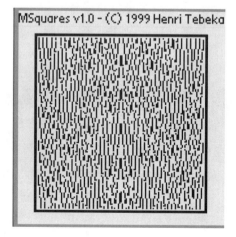

98 Store Memories on Your Visor: PhotoAlbum

PhotoAlbum, Version 3

`members.aol.com/pilotphoto`

Freeware

Take that picture of your prize-winning Labrador Retriever with you and make your Visor into a picture album. PhotoAlbum lets you do just that with bitmap images that can be high contrast (black-and-white) or grayscale (4 levels of gray). Also available is a Microsoft Windows 3.1x/95 utility that lets you create your own Pilot PhotoAlbum from your bitmap files. This is also a great way to learn the names of employees and students—and is especially easy if you have a digital camera to take the pictures (and provides even a better excuse for buying a digital camera!). Keep in mind that PhotoAlbum is just that – a tool for viewing images and nothing more.

Getting Started with PhotoAlbum

To see photos using PhotoAlbum, just click the PhotoAlbum icon and use the up and down hardware buttons to scroll through the pictures. The really cool part about this application is when you add your own pictures. To do this, follow these steps:

1. Install PhotoAlbum Studio from the CD-ROM or download it from `http://members.aol.com/PilotPhoto`. This is a Windows application.

2. Install the PhotoAlbum Studio application.

3. Click the Add button to add photos to the list.

4. Locate the photo to be used.

5. Click the Remove button.

6. Click the Create This Album button and specify the destination location for your new album (it will be named *.prc—such as photos.prc).

To install the new photos from the album to your Visor, use the Pilot Installation Tool to schedule installation of the album (called something like photos.prc).

Appendix A: Where In The World To Find All The Visor Programs You Could Ever Want

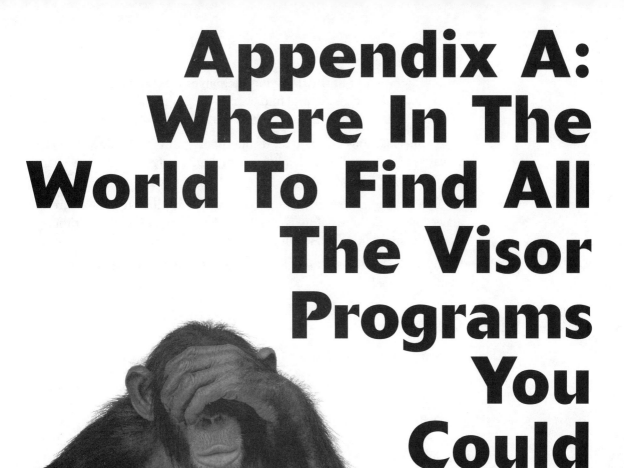

Well, if you've just finished playing Pacman or reading a Jules Verne e-book, it's time to go out and find even more programs than the ones in the book or the ones in the B-I-G chart that follows in Appendix B.

There are just thousands and thousands of programs available for the Visor because of the number available for the PalmPilot; remember, they share the same operating system.

So, here's our top five with a title and a brief description. Just make sure you have your work done before you skittle off to examine these sites, otherwise you might find yourself in Visor vertigo!

Which is the best? Visit them all and send me your vote at njs@ sunflower.com!

Visor Central

http://www.visorcentral.com

This is the central meeting place for all newbie and experienced Visor owners. Here you'll find out all about new stuff for the Visor, information on Springboard modules, articles, news, the latest accessories, and even discussion sections. A big plus for this site is the Visor News, stories about the industry and what we can expect next. And each day, there's a poll, asking Visor users and others for their perspective on topics of interest such as whether Handspring should produce a color Visor. (Who would say no?)

VisorVillage

http://www.visorvillage.com/

VisorVillage is another newbie to the stack of Visor-centric Web sites and like all the others, there are free downloads. But VisorVillage is part of PDAStreet.com, a kind of nexus for information about PDAs (personal digital assistants). You can find out about Palms, Psions, Windows CE, and other operating systems here in addition to stuff about your Visor, including news and reviews, how to articles and message boards.

PalmGear H.Q. Software Archives

http://www.palmgear.com/software/

As you already know, most of everything that works for the PalmPilot, also works for the Visor. So, it's no surprise that there are hundreds of PalmPilot Web sites that you can use for your Visor as well.

Just one of these is the PalmGear H.Q. Software Archives, where you can find more PalmPilot programs than you could ever need (no kidding) as shown by the following list of categories indicating what's available:

Astronomy	**Educational**	**MTI**
Basic	**Enhancements**	**MultiMail PlugIns**
Business	**Financial**	**Music**
Calculators	**Games Action**	**Navigation**
Clock/Calendar	**Games Adventure**	**Network/E-Mail**
Communications	**Games Board**	**OS Patches**
DALauncher	**Games Card**	**PIM's/Synchronize**
Data Input Alternatives	**Games Puzzle**	**PocketC Applets**
Database	**Games Text**	**Quicksheet Spreadsheets**
Desktop Amiga	**Graphics**	**Religion**
Desktop Mac	**Hackmaster**	**ROM Replacements**
Desktop PC	**HanDBase Applets**	**Science**
Desktop Unix	**HandScape Views**	**Security**
Development	**Hobbies**	**Shopping**
Diet/Fitness	**Infrared Apps**	**Sound**

Doc Legal	**InstallBuddy Plugin**	**Sports**
Doc Novels	**Internet**	**Spreadsheet**
Doc Reference	**Internet Palm PQA**	**TealInfo Module**
Doc Religion	**JFile Databases**	**ThinkDB Database**
Doc Software	**Language/Reference**	**Time Management**
Doc/E-Book	**Medical**	**Travel**
Doc: Schedules	**Memo Plus Templates**	**Travel/Navigation**
Document Reader	**Misc/Fun**	**TrekSounds Modules**
Download Tools	**MobileDB Databases**	**Utilities**

Once you find the category you want, click it and you'll see a listing of all the programs in that category including:

◆ the name and a brief description of what the application does.

◆ icons that you can click to download the .zip file, buy the application (if it's for sale), or open a My PalmGear Headquarters account, which puts you on their mailing list where you'll get news and special offers.

Once you click the application you want to download, you'll see an even more extensive and informative description of the file, such as the one you see on the next page.

Now you can see just about everything there is to know about this application including the date it arrived at PalmGear Headquarters, the category it was placed into, the type of program, who developed it, what you need to run it, the link to download it and how. You can also find out if any downloads have occurred just this month and forever. Especially useful is a sample screen from the application, and since a picture is really worth a thousand words, you can quickly determine aspects of the application that you might not by just reading the description. Very handy info, especially the Developer stuff, where you can visit that person's Web site or send an e-mail with just one click.

TetrisV Detailed Information

TetrisV 1.01   Add this to MyPGHQ

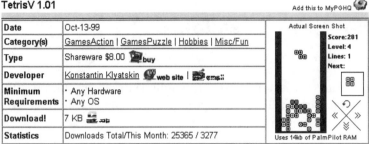

Date	Oct-13-99
Category(s)	GamesAction	GamesPuzzle	Hobbies	Misc/Fun
Type	Shareware $8.00
Developer	Konstantin Klyatskin web site	email
Minimum Requirements	• Any Hardware • Any OS
Download!	7 KB
Statistics	Downloads Total/This Month: 25365 / 3277

Application Description

Nobody beats this game! Classic game specially adopted for Palm. Now you can play 24-hours per day without your arms ached. Can be tuned both for Novice and Pro in Tetris playing.

Features:

• Incredible fast graphics
• Ability to tap control panel by stylus rather than to press buttons (much more faster and easier)
• Immediate response for input
• Next figure option (just tap a box for next figure)

There are also links to PalmPilot products, industry news, and more. This is the best commercial Web site available for PalmPilot (and Visor) downloads and if you become a Visor junkie, you'll spend hours here.

The Palm Pilot Web Ring

`http://www.webring.org/cgi-bin/webring?ring=geoff;list`

Want 631 links to Web sites that all deal with the PalmPilot and your Visor? Try the Web ring at the above Web address. A Web ring is a collection of Web sites that are all connected to one another and that all deal with basically the same content, in this case, the PalmPilot. If you want to find the mother of all Web ring directories, go to `http://nav.webring.org/#ringworld` and search for other topics and Web rings you want to discover.

This particular Web ring offers links to commercial, serious hobbyists, and about every other PalmPilot site around, be it the huge PalmGear Headquarters we just featured to the PocketBowling Homepage at `http://members.tripod.com/yhdoo/PocketBowling.html`.

What you'll find is that these sites are mostly contain programs that you can download and are a nice search engine tool to find a particular program that you might be looking for, or an application that deals with a particular topic. You'll also find links to user groups, essays on how people use their PalmPilot or Visor, and some retailers who want to sell you even more stuff than you already have.

ZD Net Palm Downloads

`http://www.zdnet.com/downloads/pilotsoftware/`

Here's the last of our recommended sites to get started with Visor stuff on the Internet. This is a huge site, which allows you to search for and download software in the following categories:

◆ Utilities

◆ Communications

◆ Productivity

◆ Travel

◆ Graphics

◆ Games

◆ Home & Hobby

◆ Docs

◆ Developments

◆ System Updates

But besides just listing categories and allowing you to download, there are featured programs, reviewer's picks, and a listing of the most popular downloads from this site. You can also subscribe to download alerts and, on a somewhat regular basis, you'll get invitations to try new programs and even advertisements for PalmPilot related goodies such as cases and styli.

We've shown you five places to get started but as the use of the PalmPilot and the Visor grows (and is it growing!), there are likely to be hundreds of new sites added to the more than 1,0000 Web sites that already exist. Have fun and come up for air to say hello to your family.

Appendix B: The Best PalmPilot Application List in the Universe

Appetite for coolness not satisfied? Here is a comprehensive list of applications that will help you maximize your Visor. Just look for the X in the last column to find the ones that are included on the companion CD-ROM; others can be downloaded off the Web. Applications with an asterisk (*) before them are discussed in detail, in the book. If a Web site is not available, e-mail the developer for information about how you can get a copy of the program.

Making Your Visor Work Even Better: Tools & Utilities

Application	Web Address	E-mail address	Description	On the CD
*Backup-Buddy	http://www.BackupBuddy.com	info@backupbuddy.com	**Automatically backs up anything that is not included in the normal one-button HotSync.**	**X**
Colauncher	http://www.mapletop.com	info@mapletop.com	**Allows you to launch applications and perform other commands with a single stroke.**	**X**
*FindHack	http://www.order.kagi.com/?4Q&S	fpillet@teaser.fr	**Vastly improves your search options and capabilities.**	
*FPS Utility Pro	http://www.fps.com/pilot/	info@fps.com	**Brings you all the important info you need to keep up with your Visor.**	
*GoType!	http://www.landware.com	info@landware.com	**Now you can enter information into your Visor as easily and as quickly as you can type.**	
*Hackmaster	http://www.daggerware.com/hackmstr.htm	helpis@daggerware.com	**Provides a standard method for managing, installing, and uninstalling system extensions.**	

Application	Web Address	E-mail address	Description	On the CD
HotPaw	http://www.hotpaw.com/rhn/hotpaw/	rhn@hotpaw.com	Create Basic programs with this scripting language application.	
PDA Toolkit	http://www.pdatoolkit.com	N/A	Create your own Visor applications–very cool!	
*Palmprint	http://www.stevenscreek.com/pilot/palmprint.shtml	sales@stevenscreek.com	It allows you to print directly from your Visor, sometimes without even attaching a cable.	X
*PalmPass	http://www2.palmgear.com/software/showsoftware.cfm?sid=68445820000112192414&prodID=5683	N/A	Track your passwords.	
Power Launch	http://www.rgps.com/	ron@rgps.com	Do you have a favorite application launcher? With this device you can program your Visor to launch it or any other application.	X
SilverScreen	http://www.pocketsensei.com/	sales@pocketsensei.com	A cool launcher!	
*Stall	http://www.tauschke.com	tauschke@tauschke.com	Allows you to install your Visor programs with just one click of the mouse.	
*SwitchHack	http://www.deskfree.com	pilot@deskfree.com	Allows you to move between two programs with a single stroke in the graffiti area.	

Application	Web Address	E-mail address	Description	On the CD
*UnDupe	http:// www.stevenscreek .com/pilot/ dodownload.html	support@ stevenscreek.com	**Removes duplicate entries with a tap of one button.**	X
WAPman	http:// www.wap.com.sg/	wap@edge.com.sg	**With this Wireless Application Protocol, you can communicate via the Internet or advanced telephony on a wireless device.**	
Word Doc Converter	http:// www.palmgear.com/ software/ showsoftware.cfm? sid=684458200001121 92414&prodID=5920	gourleyh@enersis .co.nz	**Convert Doc files to Word files, vice versa, and much more.**	
Winzip	http:// www.winzip.com	help@winzip.com	**Compresses and decompresses files quickly and easily (See the IDKYCDT introduction for more information).**	X

Organizing Everything: Databases and Information Management

Application	Web Address	E-mail Address	Description	On the CD?
AutoBase	http:// home.earthlink.net/ ~herbo/palmos_sw.html	herbo@ earthlink.net	**Allows you to keep track of maintenance on your automobile.**	

Application	Web Address	E-mail Address	Description	On the CD?
*BrainForest Mobile Edition	http://www.aportis.com	sales@aportis .com	**Management software that can be synchronized between your Visor and Windows platforms.**	X
*Gift Memo	http:// giftmemo.webhostme .com/	N/A	**Remind yourself of important occasions.**	
*HanDBase	http:// www.ddhsoftware.com/	Sales@ ddhsoftware .com	**One of the best Visor platform database programs around.**	X
*HandScape	http:// www.palmmate.com/ handscape/index.html	N/A	**Easy management and starting of applications.**	
Handy-Shopper	http:// www.palmgear.com/ software/ showsoftware.cfm?sid= 92278119990801124116&p rodID=1350	chrisant@ premier1.net	**Keep track of your shopping list and get what you need when you need it.**	X
Holiday Planner	http:// members.aol.com/ holplan/2.htm	edwards_sj@ yahoo.com	**Plan for holidays, vacations, and other important dates.**	
Magic Text	http:// www.synsolutions.com/ products/magictext/	info@ synsolutions .com	**Manipulate and organize text on your Visor.**	
Pbase	http:// hawksoft.hawkweb.com/	Techsup@ hawkweb.com	**You can keep track of information related to people in your life.**	
Pediatric Drugs	http:// www.keepkidshealthy .com/pedipilot.html	VinceI@ swbell.net	**Contains information about drugs used in pediatric medicine.**	

Application	Web Address	E-mail Address	Description	On the CD?
Pilot logbook	http://www.palmgear.com/software/showsoftware.cfm?sid=68445820000112192414&prodID=6013	Azaparov@gis.net	Great for pilots who want to log their flight activity.	
Planner	http://snafu.de/~tjawer/tjhome.htm	tjawer@bigfoot.com	Here's a graphic monthly planner.	X
Preference Manager	http://mx7.xoom.com/PixIL/Software/	pixel.il@usa.net	Manage the Visor's Preferences database by deleting items to save up memory.	
Project Planner	http://www.pathcom.com/~carolron/PDA_soft.htm	Carolron@pathcom.com	Helps you manage projects in an organized series of steps.	
*SuperList2	http://www2.viaweb.com/pilotgearsw/tapsof.html	Mfawcett@christianacare.org	Enter new items using graffiti or the keyboard, and have up to 1,000 items on a Master List.	X
TealInfo	http://www.tealpoint.com/	contact@tealpoint.com	Create and browse portfolios.	X
TealPhone	http://www.tealpoint.com/	webmaster@tealpoint.com	A fun new address book application.	X

Compute This!: A Calculator for Everything and Everyone

Application	Web Address	E-mail Address	Description	On the CD
2xcalc	http://www.geocities.com/Vienna/Opera/1910/index.html	laura.watts@usa.net	**A currency and converter calculator.**	X
Convert-It!	http://www.pe.net/firm/dpw-designs/	dpw-designs@pe.net	**Makes the task of converting between different units of measurement a snap.**	X
CplxCalPro	http://www.adacs.com/	cplxcal@adacs.com	**A graphic calculator.**	X
Dates!	http://www.enteract.com/~mwilber/	mwilber@enteract.com	**A date difference calculator that switches modes between days or weeks.**	X
DeerCalc	http://www.palmgear.com/software/showsoftware.cfm?sid=68445820000112192414&prodID=5438	rjg@lumaxlighting.com	**Calculate measurements for a Whitetail deer.**	X
Ecalc	http://www.laposte.fr/euro/	laposte@webconcept.fr	**Convert European currencies to the new Euro or other European currencies and vice versa.**	
Electronics	http://www.come.to/moelgaard	kim_maj@post2.tele.dk	**An electronics program that has color-coding calculators for both resistors and capacitors.**	X

Application	Web Address	E-mail Address	Description	On the CD
Erlang Calculator	http://www.blueneptune.com/~maznliz/marius/palm.shtml	mariusm@yahoo.com	Given a level of traffic and number of lines, this application tells you the probability of a failed (busy) call and how many lines you need.	
FuelUtil	http://www.palmgear.com/software/showsoftware.cfm?sid=68445820000112192414&prodID=4742	edwitkowski@hotmail.com	Have you ever wondered about your mileage, miles per gallon, or cost? This program can do that for you since your last fill-up.	X
Focus+	http://www.bitwareoz.com/focus.htm	bitwareoz@bigpond.com	Depth-of-field calculator.	X
*Loan Payment	http://members.aol.com/ekstrandbb/		Compute your loan(s) payments.	X
LoanUtil	http://www.palmgear.com/software/showsoftware.cfm?sid=68445820000112192414&prodID=4425	edwitkowski@hotmail.com	Calculate monthly payments, principal balance, interest, number of payments, and much more with this loan calculator.	X
LoveCalc	http://i.am/lesliet	lesliet@geocities.com	Have your eye on someone? This program can tell you the probability of it being a match.	
MiniCalc	http://home.att.net/~a.bootman/SolutionsInHand.html	solutions@hand.org	This spreadsheet has built-in math, financial, and date/time functions.	X

Application	Web Address	E-mail Address	Description	On the CD
*PalmPilot ConvertorPro	http:// www.geocities.com/ SiliconValley/Campus/ 7631/index.html	N/A	Convert from one measure to another.	
Parens	http://www.radiks.net/ ~rhuebner/index.html	rhuebner@ probe.net	A multipurpose calculator that can do simple statistics, date and time calculations, basic math calculations, and much much more.	X
*PayUp!	http:// www.portents.com/	support@ portents.com	This full-featured restaurant bill calculator computes tax and gratuity, and helps you divide the bill.	X
PilotConvert	http:// www.palmcentral.com/ product.shtml?sectionId =635&productId=1572	prestonjb@ geocities.com	Computes unit-to-unit conversions by allowing you to select from a drop-down list.	
PocketEE	http:// www.palmcentral.com/ product.shtml?sectionI d=3308&productId=4422	Portable Solutions@ ridgenet.net	A collection of electronics analysis and design tools.	
PopUp Calculator	http://www.benc.hr/ popcalc.htm	bozidar.benc@ sb.tel.hr	A convenient calculator that pops up over an active application without shutting it down first.	X
QuickTip	http:// palmpilotarchives .palmpilotarchives.com /calculators- _misc_2.html	cquick@ magicnet.net	The quickest way to compute the tip for a party of 1 to 100 at several percentage rates.	X
RomanCalc	http:// www.palmcentral.com/ product.shtml?product Id=1739	DallasKJG@ aol.com	A scientific RPN calculator with Roman Numerals.	X

Application	Web Address	E-mail Address	Description	On the CD
SavRetUtil	http:// www.palmgear.com/ software/ showsoftware.cfm?sid=6 8445820000112192414&pr odID=5754	edwitkowski@ hotmail.com	**A combination of a savings and retirement calculator in one!**	X
Scientific for RPN	http:// members.home.net/ yang2/	Jonathan.Lai .wg98@wharton .upenn.edu	**Offers most scientific functions, statistics, and linear regression.**	
ShotWiz	http:// www.shotwiz.com/	sales@ shotwiz.com	**Improve your golf game with this program! ShotWiz utilizes an aero-dynamics model that computes the best club to select, where you should aim, and how hard you should swing.**	X
Stamps	http://www04.u-page .so-net.ne.jp/zd5/ kterada/	kterada@iname .com	**Calculates needed postage based on new rates.**	X
Stock Calc 2	http:// people.ne.mediaone .net/aubin/ddt.html	aubin@mediaone .net	**A calculator for those who are investors or just interested in the stock market.**	
*SynCalc Demo	http:// www.synsolutions.com/	info@ synsolutions .com	**This is the mother of all calculators.**	X
Tipper	http://www .dentonsoftware.com/	staff@ dentonsoftware .com	**Don't know how much to tip? This calculator will let you know!**	X
Unc	http://www.flash.net/ ~marknu/unc/	gs@kagi.com	**A unique calculator with the ability to calculate in units.**	

It's Your Business!

Application	Web Address	E-mail Address	Description	On The CD
Address+	http://www .jacksonville .net/~ptaylor/	ptaylor@ mediaone.net	**Address book for your Visor with easy, convenient sorting methods.**	X
Explorer	http:// www.palmix .itil.com/	palmix@itil.com	**Allows you to explore databases between two Visors' views and delete databases.**	
*FCPlus Professional	http:// www.infinitysw .com	support@infinitysw .com	**A business calculator that allows you to compute annuities, interest, etc.**	
FonePad	http:// www.palmgear .com/software/ showsoftware.cfm ?sid=68445820000 112192414&prodID =5946	rcrespin@email.com	**Look up addresses and dial telephone numbers.**	
*IOU Mate	http:// www.PalmMate.com	IOUMate@PalmMate .com	**Keeps a record of what you lent to whom and whom you borrowed from.**	
*Lease-It!	http:// www.pe.net/firm/ dpw-designs/	dpw-designs@pe.net	**Figures out all the costs associated with your lease.**	
Life Balance	http://www .llamagraphics .com/	cewhite@ llamagraphics.com	**Balance all the activities in your busy life!**	

Application	Web Address	E-mail Address	Description	On The CD
Mobile Account Manager	http:// www.mobilegeneration.com/ products/ mobileam/	webmaster@ mobilegeneration .com	**A great way to track all your important numbers (account numbers, phone numbers, pin numbers, URLs, etc).**	
#MyCheck-book	http:// www.palmpage .com/quickster/	quickster@palmpage .com	**Your good ol' basic register that records and tracks your checkbook activity.**	
***OnlyMe**	http:// www.tranzoa.com/ html/tranzoa.htm		**Keep the lid on and keep your stuff secret.**	
PhoneDecode	http:// www.palmgear .com/software/ showsoftware.cfm ?sid=92278119990 801124116&prodID =3195	carl@ucsd.edu	**Searches out the corresponding numerals to "wordy" phone numbers.**	
***PalmQuotes**	none available	N/A	**A collection of quotes and other goodies that can keep people entertained, distracted, or whatever you need to do with words and an attentive audience.**	
PocketCall Pre-Paid	http://www .electricpocket .com/	help@ electricpocket.com	**Save up to 70% with this prepaid calling card application.**	X
Pocket-Money	http:// www.catamount .com/	palm-sales@ catamount.com	**A powerful application that can create reports, keep track of balances, and numerous other finance features.**	X

Application	Web Address	E-mail Address	Description	On The CD
*Pocket-Pareto	`http://amsoftw .tripod.com/ ppareto.htm`	N/A	**Keep track and weigh the importance of what you do each day.**	
*PostCalc	`http://dovcom .com/pilot/ postcalc.html`	support@dovcom.com	**Calculates US postal rates.**	
PunchClock	`http://www .psync.com/`	info@psync.com	**Are you working on more than one project at a time? Now you can keep track of the time you spend on each project.**	
*Qmate	`http://www .qmate.com`	sales@qmate.com	**If you like Quicken, then you will love Qmate.**	
*Quicksheet	`http://www .cesinc.com/ proddemo.asp`	sales@cesinc.com	**A fully functional tool that allows you all the functions of a spreadsheet.**	X
*QuikBudget	`http://www .QuikBudget.com`	Author@QuikBudget .com	**If you really want to stick to a budget, this is the way to do it.**	
*Stock Manager	`http:// PalmStocks .net/default.htm`		**Retrieve real-time stock prices.**	
TakeTime	`http:// www.pathcom.com/ ~carolron/ PDA_soft.htm`	carolron@pathcom .com	**Organize your billing time with a complete tracking system that records time, date, and duration of each task performed for a client.**	

Application	Web Address	E-mail Address	Description	On The CD
Time Logger/ Palm Interface	http:// www.ResponsiveSo ftware.com/	AlanMacy@ ResponsiveSoftware .com	Keep track of the time you spend with clients.	
TinySheet	http:// www.iambic.com/	sales@iambic.com	Spreadsheet for your Visor.	X
*Touchwise	http:// www.touchwise .com/	jason@ zerosixty.com	Allows trading of stocks, options, bonds, and mutual funds over your VisorSO device's network connection.	
Trans/Form	http://www .palmgear.com/ software/ showsoftware.cfm ?sid=68445820000 112192414&prodID =5459	gr3k@virginia.edu	Create forms and modify templates.	

Keeping Time: Clocks and Calendars

Application	Web Address	E-mail Address	Description	On the CD?
*Action Names	http:// www.iambic.com/ pilot/actionnames/ downloadfile.htm	sales@ iambic.com	Allows you to see all the information about an appointment in a single split screen.	X
*Alarms	www.pedos.hr/ ~kdekanic/ alarms.html	N/A	Wakes you up with such great theme songs like The X-Files, Superman, or Back to the Future.	

Application	Web Address	E-mail Address	Description	On the CD?
Anaclock	http://www.palmadd.com/	palmadd@usa.net	Here's an analog clock with a date display.	
Assistant	http://www.fiendsoft.co.uk/	gary@fiendsoft.co.uk	Both a timer and a clock.	
AvTimer	http://www.aspenleaf.com/palm/	jsimpkins@sprintmail.com	View your to-do list in the palm of your hand!	
*Big Clock	http://www.gacel.de/bigclock.htm	jens@gacel.de	Here's a free large-number-display clock equipped with alarm, world time, timer and stop watch.	X
*BugMe!	http://www.hausofmaus.com/bugme.html	iain@hausofmaus.com	Write the message, and it pops up to remind you of important events in time to get to them!	X
Countdown	http://www.wenet.net/~arajaram/pilot.html	arajaram@wenet.net	Mark a date and this clock will count down to it.	
Date Chart	http://www.palmcentral.com/product.shtml?productId=4337	malan@aloha.net	Displays stop and start times of selected events from the built-in database in a horizontal bar chart.	
*DateMate	http://www.palmmate.com/datemate/download.html	info@PalmMate.com	Automatically tracks and gives you a few days' warning before the big event.	X

Application	Web Address	E-mail Address	Description	On the CD?
*FPS Clock 2	http://www.fps.com/pilot/	info@fps.com	Everything you've always wanted in a clock but were afraid to ask for.	X
Internet Clock	http://freiamt.net/palmcomputing/	dani@freiamt.net	Internet Clock is a new global time developed by the Swatch watch people and it displays internet time, local time and a second time zone.	X
*Joke-A-Day 2000	http://www.geocities.com/larzcd/	larzcd@hotmail.com	Jokes for every day of the year.	X
Julian Date	http://member.nifty.ne.jp/washimi/Palm/Archive/Julian4En.html	washimi@miffy.club.or.jp	Shows the Julian date equivalent to the Gregorian date entered and vice versa.	
Lclock	http://linkesoft.com/english/lclock/	info@linkesoft.com	A travel alarm clock that is easy to use and has convenient big number display.	
Movie Release Dates	http://www.palmgear.com/software/showsoftware.cfm?sid=68445820000112192414&prodID=5210	bsalzer@coletaylor.com	Want to stay current and up to date on the latest movies? You can with this application that contains release dates for movies from now until August 2000.	
Mycal	http://www.nicholson.com/rhn/pilot.html	rhn@nicholson.com	This calendar helps you keep track of monthly commitments and "to dos."	

Application	Web Address	E-mail Address	Description	On the CD?
Palmzone	http://www.geocities.com/SiliconValley/Campus/7631/index.html	sjzinger@geocities.com	An easy to use, time-zone-changing application for the traveling piloteer.	X
*PhoneLog	http://www.handshigh.com/	support@handshigh.com	Helps to manage and track your phone activities.	X
Race Time	http://www.iei.net/~fraub/racetime.html	fraub@iei.net	Time and score any racing series on any size track with this.	
*Rclock	http://linkesoft.com/	info@linkesoft.com	Use your Visor as an analog (!) clock.	
Tamar	http://members.tripod.com/~YakirH/Tamar.html	hyNeni@poetic.com	A Tamar Hebrew calendar that you can also input personal dates to.	
ToDo PLUS	http://www.handshigh.com/	support@handshigh.com	Send your to-do list into high gear with ToDo Plus.	
thisDay	http://www.pointinception.com/software/	software@pointinception.com	Keep track of how long it's been since you last did something and count down to important days ahead with this handy application.	
ThisWeek	http://www.visorvillage.com/software/pc/pim.html	reesley@eclipse.net	Organize your weekly schedule with this program.	X

Application	Web Address	E-mail Address	Description	On the CD?
*TrackFast	http:// www.vision7.com/ Products/ TrackFast.asp	Products@ Vision7.com	Does the boss want to know what you did and when you did it? TrackFast can help.	
Tzones	http:// www.erols.com/ bballctaulbee/ index.html	bball@ staffnet.com	Here's an animated clock with five capabilities for five different time zones.	

Communications Anywhere, Anytime

Application	Web Address	Email	Description	On the CD
*Avantgo Client	http://avantgo.com/	http:// corp.avantgo .com/contact/ sales.html	View Web stuff on your Visor.	X
DPWeb	http:// www.digitalpaths .com/	info@ digitalpaths .com	Surf the net with your Visor.	
httpd	http:// www.citi.umich .edu/u/rees/pilot/	rees@umich.edu	Create a personalized Web server.	
IRP2PChat	http:// www2.palmgear.com/ software/ showsoftware.cfm? sid=684458200001121 92414&prodID=1883	pilotinfo@ iscomplete.com	Send messages any way you want; graphic style, text, etc.	X

Application	Web Address	Email	Description	On the CD
Mail2doc	http://user .tninet.se/ ~hhf990q/palm/ mail2doc.htm	tomas .rantakyro@ home.se	Create a Doc file with a message—a great way to bookmark and identify messages.	
MakeIt	http://xyz.com .mx/pilot/ makeit.html	dan-cocacola@ usa.net	Convert a Web page into Doc format for your Visor.	
Maple Web	http://www .mapleware.com/	feedback@ mapleware.com	Do you have trouble remembering your passwords and user IDs? With Maple Web you can keep track of them along with your favorite sites on the net.	
MultiMail Pro	http:// www.actualsoft.com/ products.htm#multim ail_professional	actual@ actualsoft.com	Easily configure email on your Visor.	X
MultiMail Discovery	http://www .visorvillage.com/ software/pc/ internet-email.html	sales@cesinc .com	Here's an E-mail application for Visor that supports IMAP4 and POP3 protocols.	
Online	http:// www.markspace.com/ online.html	webmaster@ markspace.com	A terminal emulator for the Visor organizer that connects to other computer systems.	X
PageNOW!	http://www .markspace.com/	brian_hall@ markspace.com	With this application you can send messages and much more to pagers.	X
PocketFlash	http:// www.powermedia.com/	info@ powermedia.com	Allows you to check your AOL e-mail anywhere you have access to a phone line.	X

Application	Web Address	Email	Description	On the CD
PocketBeacon	http://www.searat.com/	chris@searat.com	With PocketBeacon you can track radio beacons and much more.	
Quicksheet MultiMail Plugin	http://www.cesinc.com/qsheetmm.html	sales@cehhsinc.com	Receive completely functional Quicksheet workbooks from your e-mail.	X
TaleLight	http://ourworld.compuserve.com/homepages/mcdan/	mcdan@csi.com	An application that allows you to communicate visually by sending codes, etc.	
ThinAirMail	www.thinairapps.com	jon.baer@ctny.com	Send and receive e-mail.	
TourMate	http://www.palmix.itil.com	palmix@itil.com	Helpful device for people who need to communicate with someone who speaks a different language.	

Say What You Mean and Mean What you Say

Application	Web Address	E-mail Address	Description	On The CD
*AportisDoc Mobile	http://www.aportis.com	custcare@aportis.com	Allows you to read any document on your PalmPilot—even a book!	X
*DocToGo	http://www.dataviz.com	N/A	Convert Word and Excel documents to Visor documents.	

Application	Web Address	E-mail Address	Description	On The CD
English Explanatory Dictionary	http://www.beiks.com/	bgk@altavista.net	**An English dictionary in the palm of your hand.**	
FastPhrase Personal Edition	http://www.asycs.com/download.htm	sales@asycs.com	**Enter entire often-used phrases with a few strokes.**	
Glossary of Legal Terms	http://www.coslink.net/PalmaSrv/	PalmaServ@topmich.com	**Find out the meaning of legal terms.**	
Graffiti Help	http://www.electronhut.com/pilot/ghelp/	bkirby@electronhut.com	**It's an online graffiti reference card.**	
GroupVine	http://uc3.groupserve.com/	leland@groupserve.com	**Discuss with others.**	
iSilo	http://www.isilo.com/	N/A	**Another document reader.**	
*MIT New Hacker's Dictionary	http://www.palmcentral.com/product.shtml?sectionId=376&productId=1392	perlow@hotmail.com	**Commentary, myths, and definitions about the jargon that now surrounds the computer world.**	
*SpellMan	http://www.standalone.com/	info@standalone.com	**Checks the spelling of a Visor document and provides you with alternatives as to what word you can use.**	

Application	Web Address	E-mail Address	Description	On The CD
*Thesaurus	http://www.ddhsoftware.com/ddhthes.html	sales@ddhsoftware.com	A Palm-sized treasury of word alternatives.	X
*Thumbscript	http://www.thumbscript.com	info@thumbscript.com	System that uses a single stylus stroke for anything you can find on a computer keyboard.	X
*Translate	http://www.ddhsoftware.com/	N/A	Translate from one to many other different languages and back again.	
*WPM	http://www.ddhsoftware.com/	sales@ddhsoftware.com	Allows you to measure your word entry speed (WPM) and accuracy.	X

Lifelong Learning and Your Visor: Education

Application	Web Address	E-mail Address	Desription	On the CD
A+ Work	http://www.palmgear.com/software/showsoftware.cfm?sid=68445820000112192414&prodID=5780	rcracer@monmout.com	Easy way to keep track of your homework load.	

Application	Web Address	E-mail Address	Desription	On the CD
Doctor Doolittle	http://dogpatch.org/etext.html#swift	ardiri@hig.se	Read the adventures of a man who walks and talks with the animals.	X
*Due Yesterday	http://www.nosleep.net/	tomb@nosleep.net	Great for busy students to keep track of their assignments and performance in classes.	X
*Element	http://www.mindgear.com/element/index.html	info@mindgear.com	A simple, easy-to-use presentation of the periodic table.	X
Famous Death	http://members.aol.com/TJLivett/	TJLivett@aol.com	A huge database recording of famous persons' deaths.	X
*Flash!	http://homunculus.dragonfire.net/flash.html	homunculus@kagi.com	Presents a deck of flashcards that you create.	X
*Mahatma Gandhi's Quotes	http://www.coslink.net/PalmaSrv/	PalmaServ@topmich.com	Quotes from Mahatma Gandhi.	X
GradeBook	http://home.carolina.rr.com/adventuresahead/index.html	mdavison@nortel networks.com	Keep track of students' grades and attendance with this application.	
Hand Guide to Sharks	http://www.coslink.net/PalmaSrv/	PalmaServ@topmich.com	Find out everything you wanted to know about sharks!	
*Handy Randy	http://www.stevenscreek.com/pilot/handyrandy.shtml	support@stevenscreek.com	Handily generates a random number.	X

Application	Web Address	E-mail Address	Desription	On the CD
Herbert	`http://www.beret.com/`	`hmath@beret.com`	**Herbert helps younger children with math.**	**X**
Info USA	`http://members.aol.com/TJLivett/`	`TJLivett@aol.com`	**Find information on all 50 states including cities.**	
JungleBook	`http://dogpatch.org/etext.html#swift`	`ardiri@hig.se`	**A child raised in the jungle—what a way to live.**	**X**
LittleWomen	`http://dogpatch.org/etext.html#swift`	`ardiri@hig.se`	**Alcott's famous books about the lives of sisters.**	**X**
Memorizer+	`http://www.geocities.com/ResearchTriangle/Node/9238/index.html`	`shiyan@worldonline.nl`	**Hate carrying around flashcards? With this application there is no need to.**	
Moonphases	`http://home.att.net/~sckienle/palm/home.html#Freeware`	`PalmaServ@topmich.com`	**Records the phases of the moon 1998-2005.**	**X**
Noter	`http://www.storm.it/index.sql?section=software&lang=eng`	`support@storm.it`	**Allows you to edit music.**	
Oracle	`http://www.palmgear.com/software/showsoftware.cfm?sid=68445820000112192414&prodID=5354`	`douglasdiego@yahoo.com`	**Ask and you shall receive answers.**	
PeterPan	`http://dogpatch.org/etext.html#swift`	`ardiri@hig.se`	**Read the childhood adventures of Peter Pan.**	**X**

Application	Web Address	E-mail Address	Desription	On the CD
QuoteCalendar	`http://www.freiamt.net/palmcomputing/`	`dani@freiamt.net`	**An amusing daily calendar with funny quotes and sayings.**	X
Selected Fairy Tales	`http://dogpatch.org/etext.html`	`ardiri@hig.se`	**The Grimm Fairy tales never grow old and have a true but often grim moral.**	X
SiderealTime	`http://aslan.wheatonma.edu/~glen/sidereal/`	`gaspesla@wheatonma.edu`	**Astronomy has been made simple through this program.**	
SunFN	`http://www3.gamewood.net/mew3/pilot/rpn/`	`wilborne@gamewood.net`	**You can find out sunrise and sunset calculations.**	
The Legend of Sleepy Hollow	`http://dogpatch.org/etext.html#swift`	`ardiri@hig.se`	**Read the mystery of the headless horseman.**	X
The Lost Princess of Oz	`http://dogpatch.org/etext.html`	`ardiri@hig.se`	**This is one of the many Wizard of Oz book collections started by L. Frank Baum.**	X
Sinking of the Titanic	`http://dogpatch.org/etext.html#swift`	`ardiri@hig.se`	**Fly next time.**	X
Tom Swift and his Motor Cycle	`http://dogpatch.org/etext.html`	`ardiri@hig.se`	**The adventures of Tom Swift may have been around for a while, but are never boring! Follow the adventures of this young inventor to see what he comes up with next!**	X
World Leaders	`http://www.geocities.com/HotSprings/2382/index.html`	`xrae@hooked.net`	**Listing of world leaders and heads of state. Hello George W.**	X

Healthy Mind, Healthy Body

Applications	Web Address	E-mail Address	Description	On the CD
Anatomy 101 - Heart	http:// www.palmlife.com/ files.html	tim@ palmlife .com	Look at the human heart via six different views.	X
Diabetic Diet	N/A	bbekstrand @hotmail .com	Carbohydrate values and exchanges to aid the diabetic in diet planning.	X
Eat It!	http:// www.schereronline .de/en/eatit/	eatit@ schereron line.de	Record the foods you have eaten and Eat It! will calculate your calorie intake.	
Emergency CPR	http:// www.cprfirstaid .com/	tonyb@ netcom.ca	What to do in case of an emergency where CPR is needed.	
*Exercise	http:// pbrain.hypermart .net	sean@ smasher .com	A repetition counter for up to 9 different exercise routines.	X
Exerlog	http:// www.dietlog.com/ softcare/ exbetisher.html	softcare@ nwlink.com	Track and monitor the benefits of your exercise program.	X
Facts About Depressive Illnesses	http:// www.coslink.net/ PalmaSrv/	PalmaServ@ topmich .com	Learn about depressive illnesses.	
FDA Guide to Dietary Supplements	http:// www.coslink.net/ PalmaSrv/	PalmaServ@ topmich .com	Keep up to date on the FDA's approval of dietary supplements.	
*Food Counter	http:// www1.palmpilotgear .com/software/ showsoftware.cfm? prodID=3126	sigridw@ excite.com	Provides you with the protein, carb, and fat breakdowns of 696 foods.	

Applications	Web Address	E-mail Address	Description	On the CD
Herbal Reference Guide	http://pbrain.hypermart.net	kwillyard@mindspring.com	A health reference filled with information of the benefits of different herbs.	X
Immunization Guide	http://www.keepkidshealthy.com/pedipilot.html	vincei@swbell.net	For both adults and children.	X
Medical Sign Language	http://kwillyard.home.mindspring.com/computer.html	kwillyard@mindspring.com	An ASL medical language reference.	X
Mental Status Online Exam	http://pbrain.hypermart.net	malteser_@yahoo.com	An outline of a mental status exam.	
Peripheral Brain	http://pbrain.hypermart.net	kwillyard@mindspring.com	A collection of Memo Pad files in Memo Pad Archive (*.mpa) format that serve as a peripheral brain.	X
Pillpal	http://www.visorvillage.com/software/pc/medical.html	pillpal@ufp.com	Reminds you of your medication and vitamin dosages and the times to take them.	
*Pregcalc	http://www.thenar.com/	mike@thenar.com	Calculate the expected date of the blessed event.	X
Questions To Ask...Before Surgery	http://www.coslink.net/PalmaSrv/	PalmaServ@topmich.com	Publication that guides you in questions to ask your doctor before surgery.	
Runner's Log	http://home.earthlink.net/~martyrice/runlog/	martyrice@pobox.com	Tracks and calculates your running history.	
Smoke History	http://geocities.com/impauljs/	impauljs@yahoo.com	Are you trying to quit? This program helps you keep track of how many cigarettes you smoke.	X

Applications	Web Address	E-mail Address	Description	On the CD
SoapDish for Mental Health Workers	`http:// www.ytechnology .com/`	info@ ytechnology .com	**Log contacts with patients and this application will create a SOAP form based on those logs.**	**X**
Tacobell	`http:// ourworld.compuserve .com/homepages/ exchange/pilot.htm`	exchange@ compuserve .com	**A calorie counter for Taco Bell fast food—yum.**	
*Tealinfo Immunization Guide	`http:// www.tealpoint.com/`	contact@ tealpoint .com	**Complete source for current immunization guidelines.**	**X**
*The Athlete's Diary	`http:// www.palmgear.com/ software/ showsoftware.cfm? sid=684458200001121 92414&prodID=3111`	support@ stevenscre ek.com	**Keeps track of all the details for serious trainers.**	**X**
Workout Metronome	`http:// www.palmgear.com/ software/ showsoftware.cfm? sid=684458200001121 92414&prodID=1584`	pixel.il@ usa.net	**This counts your reps during a workout.**	

Your Traveling Guide

Application	Web Address	E-mail Address	Description	On The CD
*Abroad!	http://www .geocities.com/ SiliconValley/Peaks/ 9768/	ykanai@ m.u-tokyo .ac.jp	**Know how much money you have, what it's worth, what time it is, and the capital of where you are.**	X
AirMiles	http:// www.handshigh.com/ html/airmiles.html	support@ handshigh .com	**Tracks all your frequent-flier miles for multiple programs.**	X
*Air Travel	www.coslink.net/ PalmaSrv	N/A	**Want to know *all* about overbooking and about your rights concerning cancelled flights? A Consumer Guide to Air Travel is an iSilo document add-in and may help make those skies a bit friendlier for you.**	
Ask!	http:// www.multimania.com/ handisplay/	merlouse@ infonie.fr	**A survival flash card method of learning essentials in different languages.**	
BDicty	http:// www.beiks.com/ palmzonebg/ BDictyen.htm	BDicty@ beiks.com	**Allows you to translate from English to another language and back again.**	X
*CitySync	http://www .citysync.com/	N/A	**All you need to find out everything about your city of choice.**	
*CityTime	http://www .codecity.com.au/	DarrenB@ codecity .com.au	**Find out what time it is anywhere in the world. (This application is included on the Visor.)**	X

Application	Web Address	E-mail Address	Description	On The CD
DCmetro	http:// www.nycsubway.org/ software/pilot/	pirmann@ nycsubway .org	Here's a map of the Washington DC metro area.	
Divdiv	http://www.jps.net/ seko/main/divdiv/ div_E.htm	seko@ jps.net	Dining with a group, but don't want to get caught with the bill? This divides the dinner among group members.	
*EURO.calc	http://www.klaus.de	Klaus@ klaus.de	Enables you to convert Euro's into the local currency of 11 countries.	X
Eurodistance	http:// www.tealpoint.com/ folios.htm	contact@ tealpoint .com	This shows the distances between cities in Europe in miles and kilometers.	
Food	http:// www.moshpit.org/ pilot/	alan .harder@ sun.com	With this program you can select restaurants and categorize by food types, closing times, etc.	
GPSAtlas	http:// www.GpsPilot.com/ Atlas.htm	info@ GPSpilot .com	Download maps and this will pinpoint your location on the maps.	X
*Gulliver	http:// www.landware.com/	info@ landware .com	Keep track of just about anything regarding your next trip.	X
Hand Map Pro	http:// www.handmap.net	support@ evolutionary .net	Find where you need to go with this electronic map.	X
*Highway Manager Pro	http:// www.zorglub.com/ pilot/highway/ highway.html	cvandend@ zorglub .com	Tracks anything regarding gas and your car.	X

Application	Web Address	E-mail Address	Description	On The CD
iParis	http://www.geocities.com/Vienna/Opera/1910/index.html	laura.watts@usa.net	**A fun interactive map of gay old Paris.**	X
iTrackU	http://www.eclipticsys.com/esimain/inddiv.html	info@eclipticsys.com	**Quick way of finding out flight status.**	
MetrO	http://home.worldnet.fr/patriceb/Technique/Metro/Metro-en.html	akaiv@yahoo.fr	**Finds the shortest route between subway stations.**	
Money-Changer	http://www.lannasoft.com/	gputerbaugh@earthlink.net	**Tired of trying to convert currency rate exchanges in your head? With MoneyChanger you can do it with the press of a button.**	
New York City Guide	http://www.multimania.com/merluche/	legars merluche@yahoo.fr	**A must have for the visitor in New York City.**	
NYC subway	http://members.aol.com/larbell/pilot/subway.html	LarBell@aol.com	**A map of the New York City subway.**	
Pilots Friend	http://macinsearch.com/users/bitheaven/pilotsfriend/pilotsfriend.html	martyfhh@in.net	**Keeps track of frequencies and trip information for pilots.**	X
Placetrace	http://www.optimalvector.com/	support@optimalvector.com	**Track your mapping through GPS.**	
Sizeme!	http://www.pocketforce.com/	steve@pocketforce.com	**Helpful application for those shopping in different countries. With Sizeme! you can convert sizes for clothing and shoes.**	

Application	Web Address	E-mail Address	Description	On The CD
Street-Finder	http://www.randmcnally.com/	webmaster@randmcnally.com	No need to stop for directions with this application for your Visor.	
Travelclock	http://www.boswell.demon.co.uk/	andrew@boswell.demon.co.uk	Here's a great travel clock.	
WorldMate	http://www.palmmate.com/	info@PalmMate.com	All your travel needs in one spot, including clothing size conversions, currency, clocks, etc.	

Too Cool for Words

Applications	Web Address	E-mail Address	Description	On the CD
AlarmMaster	http://www.hausofmaus.com/	iain@hausofmaus.com	Allows you to create and personalize alarms.	X
*Auctioneer	http://www.setocorp.com/products.htm#auctioneer	N/A	Check your eBay listings as you avoid your business meeting business.	
Beep!	http://www.enteract.com/~mwilber/	mwilber@enteract.com	Extremely fun and silly sounds. Some come up just randomly.	X

Applications	Web Address	E-mail Address	Description	On the CD
Biochart	http:// www.emtec.com/ pilot/ index.html	N/A	**A graphic output of biorhythms to watch and monitor your stress or relaxation level.**	
*Biorhythms	http:// www.jeffjetton .com/	N/A	**You're at your peak (or trough)—use your biorhythms to decide whether to get out of bed today!**	
Blobs	http:// www.lfw.org/ pilot/	ping@foresight .org	**Watch the blobs go and don't let them get you.**	X
BRING IT ON	http:// www.palmgear .com/software/ showsoftware.cf m?sid=684458200 00112192414&pro dID=6113	joke24@yahoo .com	**If you've ever wanted to take your frustrations out on something, this is the application for you.**	
*BSBingo	http:// www.thisiscool .com/	N/A	**Spend your business meeting recording the ridiculous words your colleagues say. Why do you think it's called BSBingo?**	
*Cook's Companion	JEHSoft@ worldnet.att .net	N/A	**Recipes for you to add on to a doc reader.**	
*Cupidotron	http:// perso.cybercable .fr/nucleus/ pipotron/ index.html	N/A	**Declarations of love on your Visor! Web site is in French.**	

Applications	Web Address	E-mail Address	Description	On the CD
Desdemona	http:// www.mindgear .com/desdemona	desdemona .feedback@ mindgear.com	It's a board game and a great way to waste your time.	X
Diapson	http:// www.geocities .com/ SiliconValley/ 8036/pilot.html	cuendethh@ linkvest.ch	It gives the note and octave needed and is a great tool for choir directors. Only available in French, but music is music.	
Drinks	http://home .t-online.de/ home/ JoergGrohne/	JoergGrohne@ t-online.de	Who needs bartending school with all these drink recipes?	
*EasyView	http:// www.palmix.itil .com/	N/A	Backlight your Visor on and off automatically.	
*Eliza	http:// www.ddhsoftware .com/	sales@ ddhsoftware.com	Tell Dr. Eliza your problems, and she'll respond.	
Face Painter	http:// www.gollygee .com/	blocksom@ gollygee.com	A fun program where you can let your creativity run wild and paint different character faces.	
Golf Score System	http:// people.ce .mediaone.net/ rhocking/ pilot.htm	rhocking@ mediaone.net	one-four player golf scoring system that supports handi-capping, tracking gross and net scores, and much more.	X
Lovesongs	http:// www.palmcentral .com/ product.shtml?p roductId=2427	comments@ palmcentral.com	A program of classic love songs.	

Applications	Web Address	E-mail Address	Description	On the CD
Mcrazor	http:// members.xoom .com/mjmdlm	Mike_ McCollister@ msn.com.	**Turn your Visor connected organizer into an electric razor.**	X
Mirror	http:// www.utilware .com/ mirror.html	cgonline@zd.com	**Great for watching what's behind you without turning around; makes your screen go black and works as a great joke!**	
Music Words	http:// www.tealpoint .com/folios.htm	webmaster@ tealpoint.com	**Definitions for a long list of music-related terms.**	
Musician Tools	http:// www.gaisford .com/mtools/	calvin@gaisford .com	**A fun and functional set of musician tools including a metronome, a tuning fork, and the circle of fifths.**	
OmniRemote	http:// www.pacific neotek.com/ download.htm	support@pacific neotek.com	**Turn your Visor into a remote control.**	
Palm Greetings	http:// www.palmix.itil .com/	palmix@itil.com	**Send greetings to friends on their Visors.**	
Palm Journal	http://www .oncoursetech .com/	sean@oncourse tech.com	**A diary and journal in one.**	
*Piano	http:// www.snafu.de/ ~tjawer/ tjhome.htm	unitex@zedat .fu-berlin.de	**Turn your Palm into a piano.**	

Applications	Web Address	E-mail Address	Description	On the CD
Pilot-Frotz	http://www.geocities.com/SiliconValley/Way/2367/download.htm	Alien_Hunter@hotmail.com	**An Adventure interpreter for Infocom and Inform games.**	
*Pokemon Guide	www.duwa-rod.com	N/A	**Keep up with your 10-year-old!**	
Prankster	http://www.jet-ware.com/	jet-ware@jet-ware.com	**A fun application that allows you to play tricks on your friends.**	
Price Book	http://users.deseretonline.com/nalens/software.htm	billnalen@deseretmail.com	**Keeps track of prices from different stores to help you locate bargains.**	
Recipes Tried And True	http://www.palmcentral.com/product.shtml?sectionId=391&productId=2825	comments@palmcentral.com	**Cook with Recipes from the Ladies' Aid Society.**	
Scorekeeper	http://www.scruz.net/~tkier/scorekeeper/	tkier@scruznet.com	**Allows you to keep track of baseball/softball games as they are played without a laptop.**	
Sillykidssongs	http://dogpatch.org/etext.html#swift	ardiri@hig.se	**This is filled with songs kids will love.**	
*SoftGPS	Not Available	N/A	N/A	

Applications	Web Address	E-mail Address	Description	On the CD
Songs For Parents	http://www.palmcentral.com/product.shtml?productId=2379	comments@palmcentral.com	Songs parents and children alike love to listen to.	
Songs Of Innocence	http://www.palmcentral.com/product.shtml?productId=2478	comments@palmcentral.com	This is filled with songs of innocence and songs of experience. How cute.	
Starwars, The Musical	http://dogpatch.org/etext.html#swift	ardiri@hig.se	Sail into the galaxy with Star Wars. May your Visor be with you.	
*Sticks	www.beiks.com/palmzonebg/sticks.htm	N/A	Pick up sticks for your Visor!	
Sun Compass	http://snafu.de/~tjawer/tjhome.htm	tjawer@bigfoot.com	Choose between the northern and southern hemisphere and track the sun or the stars.	X
The Decision Maker	http://www.cix.co.uk/~aitches/pilot/	hfs@cix.compulink.co.uk	Have a difficult time making decisions? Use this fun random decision-maker.	
Treksounds Hack	http://aslan.wheatonma.edu/~glen/	gaspesla@wheatonma.edu	Great Star Trek sounds for you to add to your computer.	

Applications	Web Address	E-mail Address	Description	On the CD
*Useless	http:// www2.palmgear .com/software/ showsoftware .cfm?sid=684458 20000112192414& prodID=4987	N/A	Does just what it says but try it and have fun.	
*Vanity	http:// www.concepts .de/	N/A	Turn your numbers into characters.	
WineScore	http:// www.winescore .com/	info@winescore .com	Consult this program before purchasing your next bottle of wine to check its rating and quality.	X
*Yoda	http:// users.ev1.net/ ~bantha/ pilot.html	bantha@bigfoot .com	Knowledge you seek? Answers I have.	

Hours of Fun: Games, Games, Games

Applications	Web Address	E-mail Address	Description	On the CD
3 Level Tic Tac Toe	http://www.mobile generation.com/ products/3lttt/	webmaster@ mobile generation.com	Play tic-tac-toe against the computer in a 3-level version.	X
Astroids	http:// www.astraware.com/ palm/astroids	david@ astraware.com	A classic arcade game with authentic game play, cool sound effects, and those maddening alien ships.	

Applications	Web Address	E-mail Address	Description	On the CD
Backgammon	http:// www.standalone.com	info@ standalone.com	**Play backgammon against human or computer, with extensive statistics as well.**	
Big 2	http:// members.hknet.com/ ~mflo/	mflo@hknet.com	**This is a popular casino card game in Hong Kong.**	X
Blackjack	http:// www.redtailsoft .com/bjtop.html	jacobs@ xmission.com	**Play blackjack like you're at the Casino without the common limitations of ordinary computer Casino games.**	
Blackjack Analysis Toolkit	http:// www.geocities.com/ SiliconValley/Lab/ 4714/index.html	jmstoneham@ yahoo.com	**Learn blackjack analysis strategies.**	
Blackjack Reference	http://dj7.com/ liudj/PalmPilot/ Palmpilot.html	yachen@ marshall.edu	**What to do with different blackjack card hands.**	
*BlackJack Solitaire	http:// www.seahorsesoft .com/	N/A	**A timed version of Solitaire.**	
Blocks	http:// www.electronhut .com/pilot/blocks/	bkirby@ electronhut .com	**Here's a game similar to the game Tetris.**	
*Bombrun	http:// www.seimitsu.demon .co.uk/ pilotprogs.htm	bombrun@ seimitsu.demon .co.uk	**Navigate a spaceship through enemy territory.**	X

Applications	Web Address	E-mail Address	Description	On the CD
Casino	http://www.standalone.com/	info@standalone.com	**This application package includes Blackjack, Craps, Roulette, Slots, and Video Poker.**	
Casinocraps	http://www.palmgear.com/software/showsoftware.cfm?sid=922781199908011 24116&prodID=3104	jmstoneham@yahoo.com	**A Las Vegas–styled craps game with all the fun features.**	
Caverns of Kalisto	http://habitantes.elsitio.com/lpieri/	lpieri@adinet.com.uy	**Find and destroy bombs in the Caverns of Kalisto.**	
Crazy Eights	http://www.seahorsesoft.com/	jlee@seahorsesoft.com	**A matching card game for 2-4 players with several difficulty levels.**	X
Cubicle	http://members.xoom.com/PhilPilot	wattsup1@ix.netcom.com	**A 3D wire frame maze—try it but don't get lost.**	
*Dice!	http://www.palmgear.com/software/showsoftware.cfm?sid=68445820000112192 414&prodID=3041	pdamelio@home.com	**You just never know when a good game of Craps will come up—so why not be prepared?**	
Drop 'Em	http://www.standalone.com/index.html	info@standalone.com	**Arrange the tiles to complete rows to gain points. Completed rows disappear. Watch out the higher you go the faster the tiles disappear.**	X

Applications	Web Address	E-mail Address	Description	On the CD
Fire!	`http:// www.astraware.com/`	`david@ astraware.com`	**Save people from a skyscraper fire!**	
Froggy	`http:// www.pilotfan.com/ froggy/`	`tim@ pilotfan.com`	**If you liked classic arcade games like Frogger, you'll love Froggy.**	
*Frogs Vs. Cars	`http:// www.standalone.com`	`info@ standalone.com`	**The object is to get the frog across the busy street without getting squished.**	X
Galactic Realms	`http:// www.kpoole.com/`	`kyle@ kpoole.com`	**A strategy game where the object is to help resolve conflicts between new colonies as earthlings explore space.**	
*Galax	`http:// www.pilotfan.com/ galax/`	`tim@ pilotfan.com`	**Battle the space invaders with razor-sharp turns and great sound effects.**	X
HandiGolf	`http:// www.eclipse.net/ ~reesley/`	`reesley@ eclipse.net`	**Play golf on your Visor.**	
Incoming	`http:// home1.pacific.net .sg/~kokmun/ incoming/incoming .htm`	`kokomun@ pacific.net.sg`	**Defend your city against incoming aliens.**	
*Kanga.ru	`http:// www.softava.com/ silkyboard/`	`N/A`	**Lots of fun as the Kangaroo catches treats.**	
KQ: DragonballX	`http:// www.kpoole.com/`	`kyle@kpoole .com`	**An adventure!**	

Applications	Web Address	E-mail Address	Description	On the CD
Lode Runner	http://www.hig.se/~ardiri/development/palmIII/	ardiri@hig.se	**Collect all the jewels without getting caught by a guard!**	X
Lpoker	http://lthaler.free.fr/	lthaler@free.fr	**Play a casino-style poker game without going to the casino.**	
Mindmeld	http://www.rgps.com/MindMeld.html	support@exit109.com	**Break the secret code determined by your computer to win the game.**	X
Moon Rescue	http://www.seimitsu.demon.co.uk/pilotprogs.htm	pghq@seimitsu.demon.co.uk	**Fight off aliens so you can rescue stranded men.**	X
*Pacman!	http://palm.pair.com/palmpac.html	horaceho@geocities.com	**Another classic arcade game for the Visor. Gulp!**	X
Pai Gow	N/A	chrisf@ihug.co.nz	**The objective of the game is to make pairs or make nines in order to beat the banker's hand.**	
Pegged	http://home.pacific.net.sg/~kokmun/palmpilot.htm	kokmun@pacific.net.sg	**Jump the pegs until there's only one left.**	X
Place Your Bets	http://www.rosemansolutions.com/	iroseman@roseman-solutions.com	**Keep track of bets, winnings, and losses with this application.**	
Pocket Jack	http://home.att.net/~dianfrank/franks.htm	dianfrank@worldnet.att.net	**Play blackjack against the computer.**	X

Applications	Web Address	E-mail Address	Description	On the CD
Pocket Mahjong	http:// www.palmgear.com/ software/ showsoftware.cfm? sid=684458200001121 92414&prodID=1347	harrison@ asiaonline.net	A true (and very addictive) Mahjong game with Hong Kong and Mainland China rules.	
*Pocketchess	http:// www.eskimo.com/ ~scottlu	scottlu@ eskimo.com	It may not be Big Blue, but then you're probably not Gary Kasparov.	X
Poker Logic	http:// www.rgps.com/ PokerLogic.html	support@ rgps.com	A fun poker game with a logical twist.	X
Potelo	http://www.shin.nu/ ~FocV/	FocV@shin.nu	Play a new cool Othello game.	
Sokoban	http:// www.electronhut .com/pilot/sokoban/	bkirby@ electronhut .com	A strategy game where you push the blocks to the warehouse to complete the game if you can!	
Solitaire Pack	http:// www.standalone.com	info@ standalone.com	A collection of 10 Solitaire games.	X
Solitaire Dice	http:// www.geocities.com/ SiliconValley/Way/ 2367/download.htm	Alien_Hunter@ hotmail.com	A dice game for one player where you need more skill than luck!	
Tetrin	http:// www.vcnet.com/hide/ download/palm.html	hide@kagi.com	A version of the Tetris arcade game.	X
*TetrisV	http:// 195.128.67.93/	N/A	Another version of Tetris—really nicely designed.	

Applications	Web Address	E-mail Address	Description	On the CD
Texas Holdem Poker	http:// www.teleway.ne.jp/ ~kiyono/yo/ yo_top.html	kiyono@ po.teleway .ne.jp	**Here is a great poker game with great graphics!**	X
Tronic Cycle	http:// www.utilware.com/ tronic.html	N/A	**Race your tronic cycle around the field to gain points, but watch out for bombs and walls.**	
Wumpus	http:// headrush.net/palm/	bsk@ headrush.net	**Find the Wumpus.**	
X-Word	http:// www.roadkill.com/ penguin/	dpgerdes@ roadkill.com	**If you like crossword puzzles, you'll love this program that imports crossword puzzles from web newspapers.**	

What a Pretty Picture: Graphics and Design

Application	Web Address	E-mail Address	Description	On the CD
Bitmap Studio	http:// www.elucidata.com/	matthew_ mccray@bigfoot .com	**Create bitmaps with this application.**	
DiddleBug	http:// blevins.simplenet .com/palm/	mblevin@ debian.org	**Jot down notes and an alarm will remind you.**	X
*DinkyPad	http:// www.daggerware.com/ dinkypad.htm	mistered@ daggerware.com	**Ever get that urge to just withdraw from a meeting and doodle?**	

Application	Web Address	E-mail Address	Description	On the CD
Effect5	http://snafu.de/ ~tjawer/tjhome.htm	tjawer@ bigfoot.com	**A graphic effect program with drawing that has expand and collapse capabilities.**	
ePaint	http:// www.pointinception .com/software/	software@ pointinception .com	**Sketch away with this application.**	X
Escape Demo	http://www.lfw.org/ pilot	ping@lfw.org	**This program creates 3D texture mapping.**	
***FanMate**	http://www .PalmMate.com/	FanMate@ PalmMate.com	**Well, it *looks* cool.**	X
Flip!	http:// www.palmgear.com/ software/showsoft ware.cfm?sid=684458 20000112192414& prodID=974	nick@softclin. com	**Create animations.**	X
HandMemo	http:// www2.wbs.ne.jp/ ~pilotdev/down.htm	uruki@mail.wbs .ne.jp	**You can enter text and graphics in a single application.**	
Handy Pilot Font Editor	http:// www.sochi.com/ ~sandy/fe/	sandy@mail .sochi.ru	**Create and modify your own fonts.**	X
***Magic Squares**	http:// beta.homestead.com/ htebeka/index.html	htebeka@ aplio.fr	**It does nothing more than display cool animated squares on your Visor screen.**	
Neonote	http:// www.palmgear.com/ software/ showsoftware.cfm? sid=684458200001121 92414&prodID=2767	obata1@mail .wics.ne.jp	**Memo notes can be input as freeform graphics with this.**	

Application	Web Address	E-mail Address	Description	On the CD
PalmDraw	http://www.palmgear.com/software/showsoftware.cfm?sid=68445820000112192414&prodID=285	pilotgear@palmgear.com	**You can draw lines, text, circles, Bezier up to 8.5 by 11, and even use memo pads to export to PostScript.**	
***PhotoAlbum**	http://members.aol.com/pilotphoto/	PilotPhoto@aol.com	**Take that picture of your prize-winning Labrador Retriever with you and make your Visor into a picture album.**	
Pilot Image Viewer	http://www.firepad.com/products.html	mu@trends.net	**Tools that convert Pilot Image Viewer .PDB files to and from portable gray maps and portable bitmaps.**	
Piloteyes	http://www.rgps.com/PilotEyes.html	support@rgps.com	**Crazy eyes follow you on your computer.**	X
Piloworms	http://www.flex.com/~victory/pilot/pilot	victory@flex.com	**You can create simple graphics such as worms crawling across your screen.**	
Q Draw	http://www.t3.rim.or.jp/~quanta/English/Q_Draw_support.html	quanta@t3.rim.or.jp	**An object-based graphic editor that enables you to re-edit (move, resize, change order between objects, and modify text) objects even after drawing them.**	X

Application	Web Address	E-mail Address	Description	On the CD
Q Paint	http:// www.t3.rim.or.jp/ ~quanta/English/ Q_Paint_support .html	quanta@t3 .rim.or.jp	A painting software program where you can draw and use bitmaps.	X
SimpleSketch	http:// www.synsolutions .com/	info@ synsolutions .com	Allows you to draw, diagram, and much more.	
Snake	http:// weber.u.washington .edu/~billwinn/ software/ software.html	billwinn@u .washington .edu	Sample of a graphics program with this.	X
Top Gun Wingman	http://www.isaac.cs .berkeley.edu/ pilot/wingman/	topgun@abraham .cs.berkeley .edu	Looking for a graphics Web browser?	X

INDEX

Note to the Reader: Page numbers in **bold** indicate the principal discussion of a topic or the definition of a term.

MP3!
$19.99
ISBN: 0-7821-2653-7

After sex, the second hottest topic on the Web is MP3, the audio compression format that has turned the music world on its head. Create a personal music library, edit MP3 tracks, listen to MP3 files on portable, home and car stereo systems.

Evolve to a Higher Level!

"I Didn't Know You Could Do That™....," is a new Sybex series for beginners through intermediate users. Each book covers a popular subject certain to appeal to the general consumer. Written in a light, conversational style, well-known authors teach users cool, fun, immediately useful tips and secrets. Each companion CD is loaded with valuable software and utilities.

iMac™!
$19.99
ISBN: 0-7821-2589-1

See what "cool and fun" things you can do with your iMac, such as how to make movies, use it as a Recording Studio, Sony PlayStation, a fax and answering machine, and more!

Linux!
$19.99
ISBN: 0-7821-2612-x

Find easy instructions for unique add-ons, new programs, utilities for Linux, plus "insider" modifications users can make to their Linux system.

Internet!
$19.99
ISBN: 0-7821-2587-5

Discover how to see live TV, listen to on-air radio, access video vaults, eliminate spam, get help from Microsoft and other tech support resources, find the lowest airfares, and much more!

Home Networking!
$19.99
ISBN: 0-7821-2631-6

Covers dozens of home-networking projects such as connecting Macs to PC networks, connecting your TV, hosting your own web site, and collaborating on school projects.

PalmPilot!
(and Palm Organizers)
$19.99
ISBN: 0-7821-2588-3

Learn how to turn your PalmPilot into an e-book, a super GameBoy, a graphics tablet, or a music machine.

SYBEX®
www.sybex.com

SYBEX BOOKS ON THE WEB

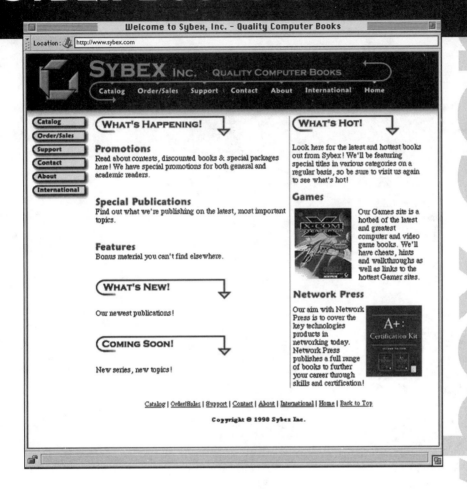

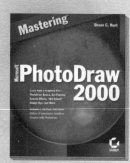

About the 155 Products on the CD

The CD included with this book contains a total of 155 shareware, freeware, and trial version products designed to help you get the most out of your Handspring Visor. Those programs marked with an asterisk (*) require OS3. The contents include:

Utilities

BackupBuddy, CoLauncher, PalmPrint, PowerLaunch, UnDupe Sample Version, WinZip

Organizational Tools

BrainForest Mobile Edition, HanDBase, HandyShopper, Project Planner, SuperList2, TealInfo, TealPhone

Tools for Computations

2xcalc*, ConvertIt!, Dates!, DeerCalc, Electronics, Focus+, FuelUtil, LoanPayment, LoanUtil, MiniCalc, Parens, PayUp!, PopUp Calculator, QuickTip, RomanCalc, Savretutil, ShotWiz, Stamps, SynCalc Demo, Tipper

Business Tools

Address+, PocketCall-PrePaid, Pocket Money, QuickSheet, TinySheet

Clocks and Calendars

Action Names, Big Clock, BugMe!*, DateMate, FPS Clock 2, Internet Clock, Joke a Day, PalmZone, PhoneLog, This Week

Communications Tools

AdVantGo Client, IRP2PChat*, MultiMail Pro*, Online, PageNOW!, PocketCall, PocketFlash

Tools to Help You with Reading and Writing

AportisDoc Mobile, Thesaurus, Thumbscript, WPM